# NATIONAL LAMPOON [R]

## 1964 HIGH SCHOOL YEARBOOK

# THE PERFECT VALENTINE'S DAY GIFT!

# NATIONAL LAMPOON ®

# BIG BOOK OF LOVE

### Edited by SCOTT RUBIN, SEAN CRESPO AND MASON BROWN

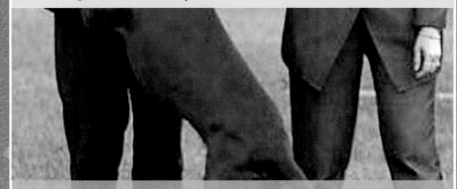

With William S. Burroughs, Doug Kenney, Michael O'Donoghue, John Hughes
P. J. O'Rourke, Terry Southern and a host of other big name talents

NATIONAL LAMPOON · 10850 WILSHIRE BOULEVARD · LOS ANGELES · CA 90024 · USA

RuggedLand

RUGGED LAND · 276 CANAL STREET · FIFTH FLOOR · NEW YORK CITY · NY 10013 · USA

RuggedLand

**Published by Rugged Land, LLC**

276 CANAL STREET • FIFTH FLOOR • NEW YORK CITY • NY 10013 • USA
RUGGED LAND and colophon are trademarks of Rugged Land, LLC.
NATIONAL LAMPOON and colophon are trademarks of National Lampoon.

**PUBLISHER'S CATALOGING-IN-PUBLICATION DATA**
**(Provided by Quality Books, Inc.)**

National lampoon 1964 high school yearbook / edited by P. J. O'Rourke
and Doug Kenney. -- 39th reunion ed.
p. cm.
"With new material from P. J. O'Rourke."
ISBN 1590710126

1. School yearbooks--United States--Humor.
2. Education, Secondary--United States--Humor.
3. United States--Social life and customs--1971---Humor.
4. American wit and humor.   I. O'Rourke, P. J.
II. Kenney, Douglas C.  III. Title: National lampoon.

PN6231.S3N38 2003          818'.602
                                      QBI03-700393

*Original Book Design by*
DAVID KAESTLE, ALAN ROSE, MARC ARCENEAUX, MICHAEL GROSS

*Updated Book Design by*
HSU+ASSOCIATES

RUGGED LAND WEBSITE ADDRESS:WWW.RUGGEDLAND.COM
COPYRIGHT NATIONAL LAMPOON © 2003

SEPTEMBER 2003
1  3  5  7  9  10  8  6  4  2

ABOUT THE EDITORS:

P. J. O'Rourke is the bestselling author of ten books, including *The CEO of the Sofa, Eat the Rich, Parliament of Whores,* and *All the Trouble in the World.* The former editor-in-chief of *National Lampoon* magazine, O'Rourke now writes for *Rolling Stone* and *The Atlantic Monthly* and lives in New Hampshire and Washington, D.C.

Doug Kenney (1946-1980) founded *National Lampoon* magazine with Henry Beard and Rob Hoffman. The inspirational heart and soul of the magazine, Kenney went on to co-write the screenplays for *Animal House* (with Chris Miller and Harold Ramis) and *Caddyshack* (with Brian Doyle-Murray and Harold Ramis).

# 1964

# kaleidoscope

# WHERE ARE YOU AND ME NOW?

## By Suzi Ruth ("Fizzie") Kroger (Fitzerman)

*C. Estes Kefauver High School Class of 1964 39th Reunion Class Historian*

Almost 40 years ago, who would have thought that, by this time, it would be 39 years later?! Talk about a big leap for Kangaroos! But even if our pouches are "paunches" these days and our "tails" are a bit thicker, we Kangagramps and grams, early Kangaretirees, spouse Kangarooters and significant Kangaothers could still hop, hop, (sock) hop for joy at our 39th reunion, although sometimes an artificial hip was involved, while Kefauver Class of '64's own Dacron Talk Radio, WANK 990, naughty-but-popular morning drive-time DJ **Wing-Ding (Herbert) Weisenheimer** spun many of our oldie favorites such as the Macarena. And lots of people were there.

Herbert just moved back to Dacron after a very interesting career as a close personal assistant to many important figures in the entertainment industry whose names you'd know in a minute. Such as John Belushi who Wing-Ding was helping with idea brainstorming on a movie script about a couple of happy-go-lucky guys who are traveling and get into scrapes, called "Road to Medellín," when Mr. Belushi unfortunately died. Wing-Ding is lots thinner than he used to be – unlike some of us "waddling wallabies" (sigh!) – and he talks even faster than he did back in high school, if you can believe it. "I'm pretty bizzy, Fizzie – got to go 'powder my nose!'" Wing-Ding quipped typically at our Reunion.

Wing-Ding Weisenheimer wasn't the only Kefauver Kangaroo who got wound up in show business. There's Class of '64's super-glamorous **Maria Maria,** star of dinner-theater stage, direct-to-video screen and local TV. We knew her when she was a regular **Maria Teresa Spermatozoa** and, frankly, a tiny bit of a Plain Jane, although always very popular, especially where boys were concerned. Little did we know that someday she would start with Lee Majors in the sitcom "MacFungo" for practically a whole television season and would be in a diet supplement commercial. Maria Maria will be playing the role of Purrrella when the Dacron Repertory Company stages the classic, "Cats," this fall. She stopped by the Reunion briefly and pleaded with us all to never go to war with Iraq again.

Reunion venue was at the VanHusen/MultiGlobal/OmnivoreCorp Arena's lovely function room, decorated in a 1964 nostalgia theme complete with a real Corvair, where the Kefauver Reunion Committee got an "Early Bird Special" discount for holding our 40th reunion one year ahead of time when there was a recession and orange terrorism alert. Catering was fancy Italian fare that had everyone saying "Calamar-velous!" and provided by **Dominic ("Dom") Brocolli,** whose Midwest-wide chain of popular Olive Pit restaurants (3 ½ Stars in Firestone Tire's Ohio Guide) have made Dom a famous Kangarestaurateur. Dom has just finished installing an indoor backyard in his new house in suburban Dacron's prestigious Gated Greatroom Acres. He also has a climate-controlled wine barn with what in-the-know wine-sipters say is the most important collection of New York State wines anywhere. Dom's "Havana Butt" cigar bar and mature entertainment nightspot is a big success, too. But Dom almost didn't make it to the Reunion when his Humvee accidentally ran over and got stuck on top of former classmate **Carl S. Lepper's** Honda Insight.

**Ddb Lzmdc ("Alphabits") O_aejk** unfortunately wasn't able to get to the Reunion at all. But she sent greetings (which got sort of garbled in the e-mail – darn my old Apple PC) from her native emerging democracy, Umbrellastan, where she is President for Life.

**Dr. Rufus Leaking** couldn't make it either. He was off on an 18-city promotional tour for his latest bestselling self-help book, "Spaz Secrets to Growing Your Personal Finances."

And **Howard Lewis Havermeyer** is sadly still dead.

But **Professor M.A. Jones** was there even though he is the busy Chairman of the Department of African-American Mathematics at top-notch Berkeley University. Fortunately, the American Association of Antisocial Sciences was holding its annual Multi-Uncultural Conference at nearby Kenyon College. And Professor Jones was able to meet and greet pals of yore at our Reunion such as **Ursula Wattersky** who was Deputy Assistant Under Secretary for Persons with Inabilities at the U.S. Department of Health and Human Services during the Clinton administration. Everyone back home in Dacron watched CSPAN with pride when she gave her testimony in the impeachment hearings about how President Clinton had always been a perfect gentleman with her even when they were alone together and were unsupervised and it was nighttime and she was on medication that may have impaired her judgment, which was incidentally probably why she couldn't remember where she put those Rose Law Firm files about Whitewater that Hillary gave her.

Although there was an embarrassing moment when Professor Jones's "high five" caused Ursula to lose her grip on her crutch and sit down on a nostalgic display of Au $H_2O$ Goldwater pins, while Ursula is running for Mayor of Dacron on the Democratic ticket. So her face was red and (ouch) so was another part of her.

What a swell chance the Reunion was to see out old (but not that old!) friends. Of course we see **Chuck U. Farley** all the time anyway with his photograph on his ad on the back of the Dacron telephone book for Farley and O'Mulligan Personal Injury Attorneys – "You May Be Injured and Not Even Know It!" 1964's Student Council ex-President just can't seem to "bound" away from the "Kefauver outback." His newest wife, Brittany, is a KHS 2002 graduate and is about to get her degree in Yoga Science from Dacron Community College.

It did this Kangabooster's heart good to see that Chuck and **Patricia Ann ("Pinky") Albright** are still on friendly terms although they have been divorced quite a bit. Patricia is a lawyer herself with the Silage County Public Defender's Office and is working hard at getting life sentences for the 26 of her clients who are on death row in Ohio right now. She is also the President of the Dacron Women's Female Forum and Vice-Chairpeople of the Ohio Choosers for Choice reproductive rights organization. Patricia says that her secret for avoiding bitterness in divorce even though she worked two jobs to put both Chuck and herself through law school at

Wayne State is effective co-parenting such as Chuck co-did every year for a weekend at Easter with their son William Kunstler Albright-Farley, who is now a successful skateboard instructor in Venice, California. In her spare time Patricia teaches a class at the Dacron University Adult Learning Extension, "Avoiding Bitterness in Divorce."

Patricia and **Wendy Ann ("Winky") Dempler and Tammy Ann ("Twinky") Baxter (Croup)** still remain the best of friends even though Wendy Ann just happens to be Chuck U. Farley's next-to-the-last previous wife! (Gosh, there were some Kanga Komplications at our 39th!) Wendy is a fitness expert and top woman athlete who would have won last year's "Buffalo Wallow" Toledo-to-Lackawana Lake Erie Swim if a lamprey hadn't attached itself to her elbow. She was in second place in the James Traficant Memorial Run for the Money Youngstown Marathon when she was attacked by a seeing-eye dog belonging to a contestant in the sight-impaired division. She would be the Gnatweight Senior Women's Powerlifting Champion of Ohio if someone had properly tightened the wing nuts on her barbell. She is currently the all-state center on the Women's Amateur Wheelchair Netball team. She runs an upper-body aerobics class at the Downtown Dacron Young Men's and Young Women's Christian and Hebrew and Muslim Association, and she is available for sessions as a personal trainer in your own home if you have a handicapped parking space.

**Tammy Ann** has been pretty busy raising the ten Baxter boys. Husband **Robert ("Flinch") Baxter, Jr.** has had a distinguished career at the Federal Bureau of Investigation. He was Special Agent on the Aldrich

Ames spy case and Agent-in-Charge on the Robert Hanssen espionage investigation. He was the F.B.I.'s supervisor for Soviet Union counter-intelligence operations in the 1980s and is currently the F.B.I. liaison for Security Affairs at the Russian embassy in Washington, D.C. Flinch says that, after 34 years of being on duty at the F.B.I., he is looking forward to retirement when he intends to split his time between a summer resort home in St. Tropez, ski lodge in Gstaad, 30,000-acre ranch in Montana and an island hideaway on St. Bart's.

Already retired is CEO and chairman of the Board of VanHusen/MultiGlobal/OmnivoreCorp, **F. George Furter,** who merged his basement silkscreen high school mascot T-shirt e-commerce business with the old VanHusen Mobile Home company to form an international conglomerate that owns California electric power grids, energy trading partnerships, an accounting firm, fiber-optic telecommunications networks, a high-tech start-up venture capital fund, an on-line day trading website with free stock analyst advice, the Kickapoo Tribe Put-in-Bay Indian Casino, and the Dacron Double-Wides professional ice hockey team.

George's wife, **Amana Furter (Peppridge),** says George expects to be paroled soon. Her husband feels terrible that he missed the 39th Reunion, she explained, because he was always the biggest Kefauver fan, not just when we were in school but right down to the present day when he earned the nickname "Kaptain Kangaroo" for attending every Kefauver home and away basketball game to cheer and applaud, especially for Kanga-sensation 7'8" Muammar Roosevelt, Class of 1999. Muammar was the only high school freshman in Dacron who drove a Mercedes S600, which he needed for its extra legroom, and he now has a famous NBA career. He kindly escorted Amana Furter to the Reunion himself. That's the old Kangaroo spirit. Hoppy sez, "Slam Dunk!"

F. George Furter wasn't the only Class of '64er to experience fortune in the business world. **Gilbert ("Univac") Scrabbler** started the first computer company in Dacron when he was freshly dropped out of Carnegie Tech in 1967. Scrabbler Electronics built early-warning radar for the USS Pueblo to use patrolling North Korean waters and night vision equipment employed by the U.S. Army at Mai Lai. It supplied vital components for the Apollo 13 moon mission, safety monitoring sensors for the Three Mile Island nuclear reactor, navigational guidance aids for the Exxon Valdez, and the entire fire sprinkler control system for the World Trade Center skyscrapers. In 2000, Forbes magazine ranked Scrabbler Electronics as the third most valuable corporation in America based on stock price. Gilbert is now living at home with his parents.

**The Reverend Bruno Grozniac** ("Lurch" to us, back when he was Kefauver's pigskin top yardage-gaining Kangarusher gridiron star) gave the Reunion invocation: "Let us never hop far from the pouch of Jesus," which he dedicated to those members of the Kefauver Class of 1964 who gave their all in the tragical Vietnam War that, fortunately, no one in the Class of '64 had to go to. But there were those of us who gave some of our all, such as the Reverend Grozniac himself, who was in the U.S. Marine Corps until his toe got infected, but not before he "saw the lightbulb" during tough basic training at Parris Island and accepted Jesus as his personal savior. Rev. Grozniac belongs to the Born-Again Bikers Veterans Association, and every year they ride their motorcycles to the Vietnam Veterans memorial in Washington, D.C., and stand there silently.

**Carl S. Lepper** also joined the military and served with pride in the National Guard at Kent State in 1970. Today he takes time off from his job as the Dacron City Health Department's Restaurant and Tavern Total Smoking Ban Inspection Officer to give motivational lectures to local youth, "Get in Touch with Your Inner National Guardsman." A self-confessed health and fitness "nut," Carl credits his energy and vim to plenty of exercise and a strict vegetarian diet. "I'm glad he's vegetarian 'cause if he comes around the Havana Butt one more time I'm gonna stuff a lit Cohiba down his throat," kidded Dom Brocolli good-naturedly.

**Angelina Annamaria Staccato** is also involved with area youth as head of Dacron's B.L.A.R.E. program to keep young people free of drug addiction and not let them sniff paint. She is well known for her lectures at Dacron-area schools where she tells students, "Don't take drugs, bring them up here and give them to me."

Many Kefauver '64-roos went into professions that service the public. **Francine Pulaski (Paluka)** is a Professional Grief Counselor, writes the "Get Over It" newspaper advice column for the Dacron Republican-Democrat, and is a member of the La Leche League enforcement squad. Her husband, Buggy Pulaski, operates the Li'l Buggers community daycare center for unfortunate youngsters, where **Father Forrest Swisher** is a frequent volunteer when he has the time in his busy schedule at Our Lady of Agony where he is the director of the Boys' Choir, coach of the Church league boys' figure skating, gymnastics and synchronized swim teams and altar boy supervisor.

And more than none of our Kefauver graduates were celebrating their Reunion with bottled water thanks to the efforts of **Purdy L. Spackle,** who heads the Dacron chapters of Alcoholics Anonymous, Narcotics Anonymous, Model Airplane Glue Anonymous, and Recovering Double Expresso Mocha-Latte-ers. Purdy is a corporate Anger Management Consultant and is also active in the Dacron Humane Society. He reminds us, "When you get into a 12-step program—and you will—be sure that one of those steps isn't on the dog."

Former Peace Corps volunteer **Faun Rosenberg** returned from Upper Revolta, where she taught village women useful skills such as how to play recorder and make local crafts into plant hangers. This gave her an idea to further do good and she started the Inner-Peace Corps, which instructs disadvantaged Dacron teens in spiritual wholeness and meditationality. She has written several magazine articles for The Nation, most recently, "Protest Songs, Played on the Recorder, Give Hope in Liberia."

Remember **Penelope Lynn Cuntz** from our days at Kefauver in 1964? Neither could anyone else at the Reunion.

**Belinda Lynn Heinke** graduated magna sorta laude from the Indiana School of Osteopathic Medicine and became a real medical pioneer as Ohio's first Osteopathic plastic surgeon. Today, the Heinke Alternative

Medicine, Chiropractic, Acupuncture, Hypnosis and Herbal Living Center graces the parking lot next to the Corngate MegaMall and offers innovative new approaches to wellness such as drive-through BoTox injections.

Heinke Herbs for Health$_{TM}$ are available in liquid and powder form in really pretty bottles at the MegaMall in **Naomi Eggenschwiler's** UniCorn Crystals and Windchimes Shop where "Eggy" has just added a day spa. When you've "shopped til you stop," drop in for one of her organic melted wax-scented candle facials and special turquoise Indian jewelry foot massages.

**Woolworth Van Husen III** got a master's of business administration from the University of the Virgin Islands and came home to work in the "family store"—that is, Van Husen Manufacturing Incorporated. But after the takeover by Frankfurter Novelty T's, Woolworth left to found the magazine Stream and Waders, devoted to salmon fishing in the Great Lakes. Many of the best stories from Stream and Waders have been collected in a book, A Cuyahoga River Runs Through It (privately printed). Woolworth was appointed by Governor Taft to serve on the Ohio Strip Mine, Waste Disposal and Environment Commission, where he is a tireless advocate of reintroducing salmon into the Great Lakes.

**Vincent Anthony ("French") Lambretta** is still a bachelor, with his "Playboy pad" in San Francisco, California's trendy Castro neighborhood, where he is as popular with the ladies as ever at Mr. Vince's Coif Creations, which he runs and owns.

But no "swinging singles" scene for single mother **Emily May Praeger,** who is a Mergers and Acquisitions Specialist and the Managing Partner at big Dacron law firm Treacle, Chromel and Doggerty, while meanwhile putting a daughter through Johns Hopkins Medical School, a daughter through Stanford Law School, a son through Harvard Business School, and another son part of the way through Juilliard Music School in New York City where he is now a rap artist in the country-western hip-hop group "Thugz on Mandolins." Ms. Praeger is also President of the Dacron Red Cross—Red Crescent—Red Buddha Association, Chairwoman of the Dacron March of Fifty-Cent Pieces, Director of the Dacron "Keep Wishing" Foundation for children who are pathetically about to die, on the board of "Paws for a Snack," which provides chewing-mouth dogs to victims of anorexia, and is active on the committees for the Dacron Influenza Ball, the Dacron Pancreatitis Ball and the Dacron Diseases of the Gastro-Intestinal Tract Gala Charity Auction. Plus, she is a prominent Dacron patron of the arts and also the crafts. Emily showed up at the Reunion with her foot in a cast, the result of a silly accident, she lightheartedly explained. She had just filled a prescription at DrugSmart when she dropped June's supply of Prozac on her foot and broke four toes.

That leaves me, **"Fizzie,"** and my love muffin with added bran, **Larry Kroger.** Larry had a long-time challenging career as mobile home loan manager at Manufacturing Creditors Trust, which he left for a big promotion to corporate Treasurer and head of the Committee for Executive Compensation at VanHusen/MultiGlobal/OmnivoreCorp. The corporate "high life" was swell (we flew in the company plane once!). But, gosh, those legal bills, and Larry now has a great new job supervising the wait-stations at the MegaMall Olive Pit.

Call me "domestic engineer," but finally the kids are out of the house at last. Jason is professionally doing well. He is one of the only three pet orthodontists in Cleveland! While Jennifer is still "finding herself." Just a week ago we got a letter from her saying, "Dear Mom and Dad, I think I might be in Seattle. Please send me money for a plane ticket to there."

Larry and I took up curling! (At age 53!) We can hardly wait for retirement (darn that stock market anyway). We've got our eye on a bed and breakfast that's for sale near Sandusky's tourist attractions. Eggy Eggenschwiler thinks "scented candles" would be a great B&B theme. Larry recently joined the Hair Club for Men.

# TEACHER AND FACULTY UPDATES AND NEWS

It is so sad to report that Mr. Rudolph Lutz, Mr. Duane Postum, Mr. Dewey Fingerhuth, Mr. Vernon Wormer, Mr. Hubbard Lunger, and Mrs. Edna Krupp the School Nurse are deceased, some of them in an untimely fashion. Mr. Martin Hackle and Mrs. Evelyn Hampster are still good at old Kefauver High where Mr. Hackle teaches Remedial Gun Control and Mrs. Hampster teaches English as Another Language. Mr. Calvin Sneedler left to go to work for NASA where he made many important contributions to the design of the Challenger and Columbia Space Shuttles. Miss Violet Coolidge and Miss Marilyn Armbruster are reported to be very happy in Provincetown, Massachusetts, where they run a small leather goods store. Miss Mara Schweinfleisch's legal troubles with deportation hearings just seem to go on and on and nobody who helped her with the ovens in ceramics class or learned how to make soap and lampshades in her crafts workshop can believe that she was ever anywhere near Auschwitz. Miss Dolores Panatella left the teaching vocation and shortly thereafter married Woolworth Van Husen III's father, Woolworth. They live in Cuernavaca, Mexico. Mr. Curtiss Dittwiley is Professor of Local History at the University of Dayton and author of the book Nothing Happened, a history of the greater Dayton municipal area. Mr. Dwight Mannsburden is Musical Director at the Ohio State School for the Deaf. Mrs. Olive Finch is retired and President of the Dacron Beanie Babies Collectors Club. Mr. Horace Bohack is Founder

Emeritus of Bohack Homewrecker Disrepair Service that has been helping Dacronians receive large household insurance claims since 1973. Mrs. Edith Girkins is now Supervisor of Sex Education for the Dacron Public School System, where she has developed the Dacron School Abstinence Awareness Programs such as "'No' Means No 'Ifs' and No 'Buts' Either" and "Keep Your Mouth Shut, Too." And Mrs. Elsa Butterick helps bring her Home Ec kitchen magic to Olive Pit restaurants everywhere as the chain Vice-President for Industrial Margarine Management.

All of us Kangantiques and Wallabifocal-wearers were heartened to see our remembered-a-lot Kefauver High School 1964 principal, Dr. Humphrey C. Cornholt. Principal Cornholt is 94-years-old but was still able to get a day pass from his extended care facility to come to the Reunion and hearten us. Although it sure was a good thing for him that he had the oxygen tubes up his nose when that really, really gross thing was found floating in the punch bowl! But otherwise it was a night to not forget.

So goodbye for now and see you in 2043 for our 79th! Better start making those motel reservations now!

*Kanga - Kisses!*

*Fizzie!*

## A Letter From Dr. Humphrey C. Cornholt, Principal, C. Estes Kefauver Memorial High School

*Dear Mr Kroger,*
*The only true human*
*waste is waste of*
*time. Regards,*
*H. Cornholt*

Dear 1964 Graduating Class of C. Estes Kefauver Memorial High School:

Now, at the tail end of my first year on the Principal's stool at Kefauver High, certain thoughts begin to emerge and I would like to pass a few of these along to you.

First, graduation can be viewed as one of two things: a beginning or an ending. Indeed, there are some here to whom graduation will be a finale, a closing of both the schoolbooks and the mind. It is not to them that I speak. Rather it is to those who are determined to continue the educational strain, to push ahead, and to digest more and more "food for thought" each day.

Second, I'd like to say that it gives me great pleasure to be able to release all that I've been holding inside me so long, and to tell you what a nice feeling it has been for me to perform my duties as Principal among such firm and regular young people as you.

Third, let me, if I may, use this "rest stop" in the *Kaleidoscope*'s busy action to sound just a few notes about the kind of world you and your fellow students are entering as you come out at the end of your journey through our educational system. Let me extend a few pieces of solid advice to aid you in finishing those things which we must all, by nature, finish and to assist you in eliminating, in as smooth and easy a manner as possible, those things in life which must be eliminated.

A great philosopher once said, "It is the silent doer who makes the cent while the wind-bag critic ends up with mud in his eye!" And, indeed, today's world is flush with opportunities awaiting that silent doer's plunge. But to succeed you must know *what* you are doing and *where* you are doing it. You must bear down hard as you can during every task; and, no matter what the outcome, wipe your slate clean afterwards. Should the world confront you with a price to pay, pay it proudly. Then turn the lock, open the door, and let loose your all! And if accidents happen, always remember that "Today's waste may be the morrow's taste." Beware of those who would hurry you needlessly and of those who would exert a constipating influence. Fertilize the minds of those you pass and the grounds on which you tread. Leave the droppings of wisdom and those who are awaiting behind will follow the trail. Shun hot air when there's nothing solid behind it. And, in mind and body, heed nature's call and keep "all systems GO."

And this is what I leave you with, Seniors of 1964; only let me make one final comment about the teaching profession of which I, of course, am a part. It is my personal reply to the old saw we've heard so often, that "Those who cannot do, teach." My answer to that is solely in the examples I set whereby I hope to have proven to you that some of us in the world of education can "do" quite well after all!

I remain very truly yours,

*Humphrey C. Cornholt*

Dr. Humphrey C. Cornholt
Principal, C. Estes Kefauver
Memorial High School

# C. ESTES KEFAUVER
# MEMORIAL
# HIGH SCHOOL

"EX · LIBRIS"

# DACRON, OHIO

# Kaleidoscope

# Nineteen Sixty-Four

# Contents

# DEDICATION

### John F. Kennedy
### 1917-1963

We proudly dedicate the 1964 *Kaleidoscope* to John Fitzgerald Kennedy, whose tragic death marred the passage of this year at Kefauver High, a man whom we admired not for what he did for himself but for what he did for his country and we as citizens of it.

JFK, perhaps we learned more from you than from any other teacher in high school. You taught us the courage of action in West Berlin, the wisdom of patience in Southeast Asia, the action of wisdom in our space race, the patience of courage in desegregated schools, and the active patient wisdom of wise courageous action at the Guantánamo Naval Base. You are gone, but you have left behind a legacy of peace and prosperity at home, abroad, and in school. And, though the Presidency has passed on to other able hands, it is you who remains "President of the Class of '64" in our hearts. You who might as well have said, *"Ich bein ine Kefauver Senior."*

FACULTY & ADMINISTRATION

# ADMINISTRATION

## A Message from Philo M. Doggerty, Superintendent of Schools

### A Message from Assistant Superintendent of Schools Durward Chromel

Congratulations to all Dacron School System Graduating Seniors, and I know how proud you are to be receiving them. Let me take a moment to leave you with a thought I have found very valuable to my success down through the years: That is, that now when you are leaving your respective high schools, do not be mistaken and think you have left school behind. For, in fact, you are now about to enter the largest school of all. And I am not speaking of even Ohio State, where some of you will have the good fortune to go, but of the School of Life. Yes, for all of life is a school. Your classrooms will be your jobs and professions, and our country's elected officials and the respected business and religious leaders of our communities will be your faculty and administration. Perhaps exams will not be held on so regular a schedule, perhaps grades will not be posted exactly four times each year, but exams there will be and your "grades" will be posted for everyone to see. Indeed, you will find all of school in life—the homework it takes for success, the surprise quizzes when sudden problems arise and require your mature judgment, the "school spirit" you'll show for America itself, and even the enjoyable extracurricular activities of your future families and social get-togethers.

So have a good time at your graduation ceremony and be rightfully proud of your accomplishments. But don't forget that the next "school bell" that rings will find you "in class" for the "required course" in Adulthood, where the tests you're given will determine your future forever!

Congratulations, Graduating Seniors, and let me offer a small piece of advice: You are leaving high school but you are entering "Life School." Instead of classrooms, you'll have offices and factories. Instead of teachers, you'll have superiors and supervisors. But everybody will still know what kind of grades you're getting. So be glad that you've passed in high school but remember not to flunk your future.

*Dacron Board of Education*: Morton Treacle, *President*, Marie Corning, *Secretary* Shelton Polk, Irwin Dewlap, Samuel Quiggs, Conrad Hobble, L. Philip Gerwin.

# FACULTY

**Mr. Martin Hackle**
**Mathematics.** Bob Jones University; B.S. Adviser: Slide-rule Club, Square Rooters. Sponsor: Annual Mix 'n' Math dinner dance.

**Mrs. Evelyn Hampster**
**English.** St. Catheter's College; B.A. Dramatics Coach. Adviser: *Prism*, Esperanto Club. Sponsor: *Leaf and Squib*.

**Mr. Calvin Sneedler**
**Chemistry, Physics.** Ball State Teacher's College; B.S. Boys' Dean. Adviser: Rocketry Society, Atomic Bomb Club.

**Mr. Rudolph Lutz**
**Biology, General Science.** Tuskegee Institute; B.S. Adviser: Jr. Red Cross/Red Feather, Fetal Pig Club.

*To Señor Larry*
*Recuerda las palabras*
*Entiende el mundo!*
*Buenos Suerte*
*Señorita Panatella*

**Miss Dolores Panatella**
Romance Languages. Canal Zone Jr. College; B.A. Adviser: Future
Stewardesses, Piñatas y Sombreros.

**Mr. Curtiss Dittwiley**
History, Social Studies. Florida Normal; B.A.
Adviser: Debating Society, Tidy Lawn Squad.

**Mr. Duane Postum**
Health, Driver's Education. Sheetrock State Teacher's
College; B.A. Coach: Basketball, Track. Adviser:
Boys' Hygiene Club. Sponsor: Senior Class Trip.

**Mr. Dewey Fingerhuth**
Latin. L'Acadamie Nationale de Serbo-Croatia; A.M.B. Adviser:
Society for the Appreciation of the Ancient Classics. Sponsor: Arbor
Day Pliny Recital.

# *Through Each Test and Trial...*

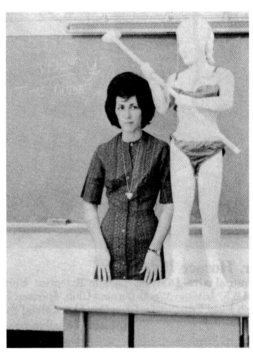

**Miss Mara Schweinfleisch**
**Art.** Barbizon School; B.F.A. Adviser: Clay Pot Club, Yarn Club. Sponsor: Sophomore Orphans' Puppet Show.

Don't B #
Don't B ♭
Just B ♮!
Mr Dwight
Mannsburden

**Mr. Dwight Mannsburden**
**Music, Music Appreciation.** Longine Symphonette Conservatory of Music; M.F.A. Director: Marching Band, Mixed Chorus. Adviser: Tuba Club, Future Optometrists.

**Mrs. Elsa Butterick**
**Home Economics.** Air Force Institute of Technology; B.S. Adviser: Future Housewives, Dusting Club. Sponsor: Senior Porridge Sale.

**Mrs. Edith Girkins**
**Sex Education.** Ossining State University; B.A. Water Ballet Coach. Adviser: Girls' Hygiene Club.

# To Kefauver Give

## Mrs. Olive Finch
**Business Skills.** Harvey Mudd College; B.A. Coach: Typing Team. Adviser: *Kaleidoscope*, Junior Achievement. Sponsor: Senior Mothers Dictaphone Tea.

## Mr. Horace Bohack
**Industrial Arts, Drafting.** LaSalle Extention University; B.S. Adviser: Wood-Burning Club. Sponsor: Earl Sheib Field Trip, Senior Class Day Sheet Metal Band.

## Miss Marilyn Armbruster
**Girls' Physical Education.** Purdue University; M.A. Girls' Dean. Coach: Bowling Team. Adviser: Hall Monitors, Smoking Patrol, Luncheon Sentinels, Walkway Safety Guards, Junior Police.

## Mr. Vernon Wormer
**Boys' Physical Education, Civics.** Texas Baptist Tech; B.A. Coach: Football, Wrestling. Adviser: Life Scouts, Varsity Club. Sponsor: Varsity Club Annual Benefit Track Meet with Dacron Retarded Children's Shelter.

# Service with a Smile

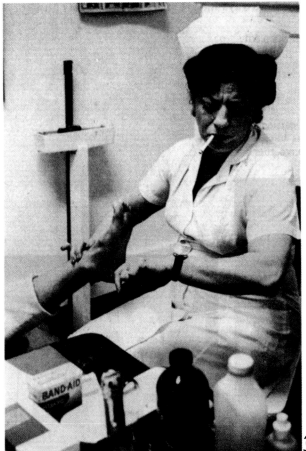

**Mr. Hubbard Lunger**
Career Counseling. Baldwin-Wallace; B.A., Parsons College; M.A.

**Mrs. Edna Krupp**
School Nurse. Sorghum State Agricultural College; B.Ed., R.N.

**Miss Violet Coolidge**
School Librarian. Moody Bible Institute; B.A., M.L.S. Adviser: League for Literary Uplift.

# And Lest We Forget

. . . the "little people" who also make "big" contributions to Kefauver High in their own small way. Whether mopping a dirty floor, driving a stinky old bus, cleaning up vomit and vandalisms, or simply handling our foods, these valuable and wonderful people will always have a place in our hearts and buses and basements as long as they live.

To them we truly and sincerely say "hats off" and "thanks a lot."

# Food Services

Like cars that run on gasoline, active KHS learners get "motorvation" from well-balanced and nutritious luncheons prepared with care by others so that we will have fuel for sports, dating, and memorizing ideals.

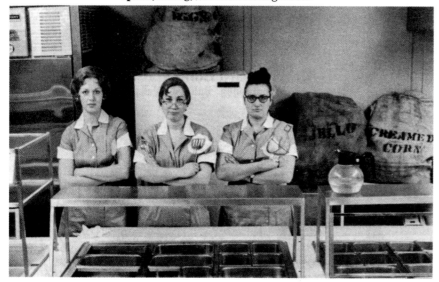

*Left to right:* Dorene Milner, Eleanor Lubitz, Velma Prawn.

*Left to right:* I. Tronley, M. Nesbitt, P. Grommet.

# Custodial Engineers

Janitorial duties around KHS may not be as challenging as teaching students about space-age technology and the real world around us, but how many of us could drive a spaceship if the cockpit were full of unpicked-up floating litter and garbage? Food for thought.

*Left to right:* Stanislau Dupa, *Superintendent;* Norton Weevil, *Assistant Superintendent;* Humbolt C. Cornfrey, *Temporary Lavatory Maintenance.*

Dear Larry

Well, it's hard to "leave the pouch" but we all had so many oodles and oodles of real blasts it's a wonder most of us still got mostly A's and B's! These past 4 years were the best of my life and I'm sure they will be for you, too! Go Kangaroos!!!

Always,
Suzi!

P.S. I still don't have your Pep Club dues yet. C'mon, cough up!

# Seniors

what a
dipshit!
—wmyDing

# In Memorium

Of all the pieces that are appearing in this, the *Kaleidoscope* of this year, this is, I am sure the saddest piece you will read and one of the hardest ones to write. As I sit here at my binder in the Yearbook Room, trying to think of what would be the right words to say, I realize that trying to say the right things about a thing like this is as hard as trying to get up in Mrs. Hampster's English class for one of her famous oral talks when she doesn't give you the topic until you're up in front of the class, and so you usually just say stupid things that you wish you weren't saying.

What I have to write about here is one of our students who is no longer with us, if you know what I mean, and it's not that he transferred or flunked out. His name was Howard Lewis Havermeyer, and most of us here on the *Kaleidoscope* staff didn't get a chance to know him too well because even when he did come to school, he coughed a lot and sometimes after coughing he made funny noises, and someone once said that Nurse Krupp told our parents that we shouldn't stand too close to him even when he wasn't coughing.

But just because we did not know him, however, does not mean that he was not a real nice guy. He used to smile at people when he wasn't coughing, and he was supposed to have been really good at baseball when he wasn't coughing. He was supposed to be good at swimming too, and he would have made the swimming team for sure if the county had given Coach Wormer permission to make the water warmer. They say he was even supposed to have been good at touch football, although he was supposed to stay away from dust, and a lot of the girls thought he looked like a Master of Ceremonies.

As I said, there isn't anything much a person can say about something like this. We all would have been a lot happier if he were still here among us, and what happened to him was certainly a bad mark on all the happy events of our young years. We had a wonderful time

## Patricia Ann Albright
### "Pinky"

*"People, people who need people . . ."*
Sweet, peppy, and cute . . . "What a riot!"
. . . dozens of scrapbooks . . . "That's
really sweet!" . . . mad about: plaid . . .
"No? You're *kidding!*" . . . pet peeve:
homework . . . big heartthrob: Chuck
Farley . . . thinks Paul's the cutest . . .
"Darn!"

Kangarooters 3,4; Kangarooterettes 1,2;
Student Council Representative 1,3; J.A. 4;
Pep Club 1,2,3; Chairman, Pep Club Assembly; One Minute Root 4; Junior Class Secretary 3; Sophomore Class Treasurer 2; *Prism*
2,3,4; *Kaleidoscope* 3,4; Senior Skip Day
Sub-Chairman 4; Kefauverarians 2,3, Secretary-Treasurer, 4; Public Address System
Good Cheer Squad 2,3; Pesterettes 1,2,3,
President, 4; Kang Kang Dancers, Evening
in Paris Talent Night 2; Junior Jumpers 1,2;
Candy Striper 3,4; Kefauvereens 1,2,3,4;
Boosteroos 3,4.

## Dominic Xavier Brocolli
### "DOM"

*"Do unto others before they do unto you"*
Black pegged chinos . . . '58 Mercury
turnpike cruiser . . . "You wish" . . . lights
"flamers" in study hall . . . "Ask me if I'm
a turtle!" . . . a diamond in the rough . . .
"I was only resting my eyes" . . . pulls
some real boners . . . guinea gliders . . .
manually-minded . . . I'll get down on
my knees if you'll get down on your
elbows!" . . . pocket pool champ . . .
"You're hired!"

Winner Annual Freshman-Sophomore
Kanga-Roughhouse 1,2; Manual Arts Club
1,2,2,3,3,3,4,4.

## Robert Baxter, Jr.
### "Flinch"

*"A square peg in a square hole"*
Neat, dependable, regular guy . . . sincere, clean-cut, forthright, upstanding,
down-to-earth, straight shooter, square
dealer, well-rounded, well-groomed,
well-liked . . . "Keep it clean, there're
girls around!" . . . a Kangaroo for all seasons . . . terrific gun collection . . . pet
peeve: people who are always trying to
be "different" . . . saving himself for marriage . . . all man, all-American, A-OK
. . . a future astronaut!

Explorer Scouts 2,3,4; Kiwanis Citizenship
Award; Varsity Football 2,3, Capt.,4; Rotary
Patriot's Citation; Varsity Basketball 2,3,
Capt., 4; Shriner's Community Service
Plaque; National Honor Society 3,4; Varsity
Track 2,3,4; Elks' Achievement Commendation; Moody Sportsmanship Trophy; Kangarangers 1,2,3,4; Moose Memorial Men's
Merit Mention; World Youtheran Leadership Council; Kangarooter -Backers 1,2,3,4;
Friendly Order of Eagles "Silver Beak";
Kangarooter -Backer -Boosters 1,2,3,4; Second Alternate West Point Designate; Masonic Lodge Responsibility Ribbon; National
Rifle Association; Future Veterans of Foreign Wars.

## Tammy Ann Croup
### "Twinky"

*"People who need people are the
luckiest people . . ."*
Neat, cute, and pert . . . "Oh, ick!" . . .
million photos in her wallet . . . "Are you
for real?" . . . mad about: matchables . . .
"Let's not and say we did" . . . pet peeve:
pesky little brother . . . stars in her eyes
for: Bob Baxter . . . John yeah, yeah,
yeah . . . "That's really cute!"

Kangarooters 3,4; Kangarangers 1; Kangarooterettes 2; Pep Club 1,2,3,4; Homeroom
President 2; Senior Class Secretary 4; *Prism*
3,4; *Kaleidoscope* 2,3,4; Chairman Spring
Kanga-Karnival Handshake Booth 3; Kefauverillians 2,3; Christmas Poverty Poor Folk
Perk-Up 1,3; P.A. Prattlers 3,4; New Student Welcome Locker Committee 3,4; Jumperettes 1,2,3,4; Young Kefauverians 2,3,
President, 4; Co-chairman, Sophomore Hay
Walk 2; C. Esterettes 1,2; Junior Bake Sale
Ticket Committee 3.

## Penelope Lynn Cuntz
### "Penelope"

*"Let a smile be your umbrella"*
Good listener . . . attractive smile . . .
shy type . . . pleasant grin . . . still waters that probably run deep . . . a smile
for all . . . "Excuse me" . . . cheerful
smile . . . attentive listener . . . quietly
silent . . . a real cute smile.

Perfect Attendance Club 3.

**Naomi Eggenschwiler**

**"Eggy"**

*"I enjoy being a girl"*

Giggles galore . . . cute in culottes . . . screen thrill: Beach Party Gang . . . Larry, Larry, Larry, Larry all over her notebooks . . . Nash Metropolitan—Mr. Beep-Beep . . . loves puppies and kittens . . . favorite color: pink . . . "Hi!!!" . . . pajama parties . . . mushy for crushes . . . mad for: fluffy sweaters.

Typing Team 3,4; First Prize, Ohio State Crisco Fry-Off 4; Oven Club 2,3.

**Franklin George Furter**

**"Gopher"**

*"They also serve who only stand and wait"*

One thing he's not short on is school spirit . . . a big athletic supporter . . . "One towel to a customer" . . . snipe hunts . . . "Hey, guys, wait up!" . . . pantsed in the girls' gym . . . "Aw, come on, cut it out" . . . "Hey, no kidding, that hurts!" . . . "Ouch, quit it will ya, ow, ow, ow . . ."

Football manager 1,2,3,4; Basketball manager 2,3,4; Track Manager 2,3,4; Locker Room Pick-Up Squad 1,2; Bat Boy All-City Baseball Team 4; Girl's Volleyball Mascot 3; Spirit Week Litter Chairman 2; Pouchkateers 2,3, Secretary, 4.

**Charles Ulmer Farley**

**"Chuck"**

*"Shoulder to the ground, feet on the ball"*

Firm handshake for all . . . most likely to succeed . . . pleasant word for all . . . "Call me Chuck" . . . wing tipped cordovans . . . real go-getter . . . carries lunch in briefcase . . . convincing smile for all . . . executive-length boxer shorts . . . "Let's have lunch period together real soon!" . . . guy on the go . . . Mr. Popularity . . . Au H₂O!

Varsity Football 2,3, Co-capt., 4; Student Council Pres. 4; Varsity Basketball 2,3,4; Class Pres. 1,2; Varsity Putters 1,2,3, Capt., 4; JA 1,2,3,4; Young Ohioans Young People's Youth League; Good Citizenship Committee 2,3,4; Dacron Area Student Council Representative; Young Americans for Freedom; Future Political Science Majors 4; Glad-Handers 1,3,4; Future Officeholders 2,3, Pres., 4; Kanga-Young-Republicans 1,2,3,4; Future Real Estate Speculators 1,2,3,4.

**Suzi Ruth Fitzerman**

**"Fizzie"**

*"Be true to your school"*

Vim, vigor, and vitality! . . . pert, neat . . . Gidget goes to KHS . . . alert, petite . . . color me turquoise and orange . . . flirt, sweet . . . heartthrob: Vince Edwards . . . squirt, tweet . . . mischievous little minx . . . "Too pooped to pop!" . . . chatterbox . . . sleeps in her Kangaroo suit.

Kangarettes 1,2,3,4; Kangarooter–Boosters 1,2,3,4; Kangarangerettes 1,2,3,4; Kangarooter-Booster-Backers 1,2,3,4; Pep Club 1,2,3,4; Boosteroos 1,2,3,4; Walla-Baby-Sitters 1,2,3,4; Sr. Helperettes 1,2,3,4; Pouch 'n' Paw 1,2,3,4; Hopperettes 1,2,3,4; Jr. Jumpers 1,2,3,4; Girls' Aqua-Hockey 1,2,3,4; Girls' JV Lawminton 1,2,3,4; Girls' Shuffleball 1,2,3,4; Dacron General Hospital Candy-Striper; Kanga-Rinos Girls' Auxiliary 1,2,3,4.

**Wendy Ann Dempler**

**"Winky"**

*"But first, be a person who needs people . . ."*

Pert, sweet, and peppy . . . "Mind your own beeswax!" . . . bedroom *full* of stuffed animals . . . "Great!!!" . . . mad about: madras . . . "Let's not spoil it" . . . pet peeve: cleaning her room . . . dream date: Chuck Farley or Bob Baxter . . . Ringo, Ringo, Ringo . . . "Neat!"

Kangarooters 4; Kangaroosters 1,2,3; Pep Club 1,2,3,4; Junior Class President 3; Student Council Sergeant-at-Arms 2,3; *Prism* 3,4; *Kaleidoscope* 3,4; Y-Teens Volunteer Orphan's Rummage Drive 3; Kefauverettervillianeens 2,3,4; Senior Sweat Shirt Day Bid Committee 4; Chairman Sophomore Root Beer Blast 2; Future Mothers of Children 1,2,3; Young Men and Moms Date Dance Decorations 3,4; Faculty Lounge Usherette 2,3; Key-Fauveers 2,3,4; Varsity Golf Whisperette Rooters 3,4.

**Bruno Walter Grozniac**
"Lurch"
*"He's kind of big and he's awful strong"*
"Baby Huey" . . . pink bellies . . . calls a spade a spade . . . Dutch rubs . . . "Whadda fruit!" . . . Deep Heet in Zippy's jock . . . Indian burns . . . chug-a-lugger . . . "Huh?" . . . crushes beer kegs with one hand . . . pantsed Gopher in girls' locker room . . . rips phone booths in half . . . "Wanna mouthfulla bloody Chicklets?" . . . future Green Beret.

Varsity Football 1,2,3,4,4; Varsity Wrestling 2,3,4,4; Varsity Lacrosse 1,2,3; Varsity Punching 3,4; Varsity Weight Lifting 3,4; Student Court Executioner.

**Madison Avenue Jones**
"Zippy"
*"All men should be created equal"*
Newcomer from Nashville Lincoln Roosevelt . . . stands out in a crowd . . . "Yassuh" . . . "Shore nough" . . . "Dat's right, Boss" . . . exciting first year at KHS . . . fast on his feet . . . tenor for the "Suede Tones" . . . sure can sing, dance, run, and play baseball . . . a credit to his homeroom.

Football 4; Basketball 4; Wrestling 4; Track 4; Baseball 4; Intramurals 4.

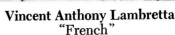

*Larry—*
*Remember, they're all the same upside down and that went for Twinky, too!*
*One who knows,*
*French*

**Vincent Anthony Lambretta**
"French"
*"He's good bad but he's not evil"*
Continental clothes . . . can do fast dances . . . wavy hair . . . Grecian nose and roamin' hands . . . "BT" . . . "Beaver" . . . octopus arms . . . candy-apple red 409 . . . blue make-out lights under the dash . . . button-tufted white naugahyde wheel wells . . . nose for nooky . . . "If I told you you had a good body would you hold it against me?" . . . riding bareback . . . "It's all pink on the inside."

Football 3,4; Basketball 4; Kar Klub 1,2,3,4; Kangaccordianaires 2,3; 4F Club 2,3,4.

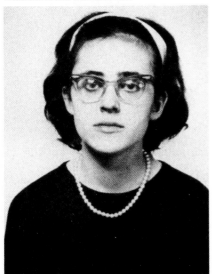

**Belinda Lynn Heinke**
"Metal Mouth"
*"Knowledge is in the ear of the learner"*
Intelligent but nice . . . neat handwriting . . . on the quiet side . . . lots of study dates . . . sensible shoes . . . really out of it.

Perfect Attendance Club 1,2,3,4; Honor Roll 1,2,3,4; National Merit Finalist; Valedictorian; 100 Grade Average; National Honor Society 1,2,3,4; KHS $100 Moody Memorial Scholarship; Slipsticks 1,2,3,4; Homework Club.

**Lawrence Kroger**
"Larry"
*"A man never stands so tall as when he stands on his own two feet"*
Nice guy . . . lives close to school . . . Sunnyrock quarry surfer crowd . . . "Hot Dog" . . . "Wahine" . . . "Hang Ten" . . . grounded a lot . . . Dad's Lark . . . "Shotgun!" . . . stuck on Twinky C . . . WOIO Oldies Week—lots of "Tammy" requests . . . mows lawns in the summer.

*Prism* Sales 2; JV Football 3,4; Track 2,3,4; Intramural Touch Wrestling 2,3; Audio Visual Aids 1,4; Rocketry Club 4.

### Carl S. Lepper
### "Fungus"

*"Absence makes the heart grow fonder"*
A watchful guardian of KHS tradition . . . beady little eyes . . . "Let's see your hall pass" . . . Cornholt's Commandos . . . "Detention Study Hall is full of guys like you" . . . greasy kid stuff—on his nose and cheeks! . . . Dad works for the IRS . . . volcano face . . . Summer job as a drive-in movie attendant.

Hall Monitors 1,2,3, Lieutenant Colonel 4; Junior Police 2,3,4; Chairman, Locker Safety Week 3; Lavatory Patrol 2,3; Gym Showering Monitor 2,3; Student Court Prosecutor 4; Lunch Tray Chaperon 1; Bay of Pigs Club 3,4; Tidiness Committee 1,2,3,4; Walk-Way Proctor 2,3,4.

### Rufus Leaking
### "Spaz"

*"Shake, rattle, and roll"*
Easy-going . . . always on the move . . . happy-go-lucky . . . smile for everything . . . carefree . . . can take a joke . . . great dribbler . . . stores erasers in his cheeks . . . good sport . . . ants in his pants . . . forever blowing bubbles . . . brown hair, wavy eyes.

Remedial English 1,2,3,4; Therapeutic Numbers 3; Special Students Club 1,2,3,4; Flash Card Club 3; Slow Learners Council 2,3, Pres., 4; Corrective Speech 2; Breathing for Credit 4; Finger Paints 3.

### Francine Paluka
### "Half-Track"

*"Poetry in motion"*
Strong silent type . . . big Paul Hornung fan . . . "You eat with that mouth?" . . . tag team matches in the girls' locker room . . . "Watch yer language, Bud" . . . knitted barbell booties . . . "Listen, fresh guy, want your face redecorated?" . . . keeps 'em quiet at the Y-Teen dances . . . headed for Purdue.

Girls' Field Squash Captain 2,3,4; Girls' Gym-Ball Captain 2,3,4; Girls' Tennis Mitten Captain 2,3,4; Girls' Hurdle Hockey Captain 2,3,4; Most Outstanding Senior Athlete 4.

### Ddb Lžmdc Oûaejk
### "Alphabits"

*"Bring us the wretched refuse of your teeming shore"*
Kefauver's first AFS student . . . hands across the sea . . . combs her hair with a fork . . . rubs Reese's peanut butter cups into her clothing . . . "Is not for eating this round meat stitched with sewing as the yak bladder stuffed of elm leaves my country good yum?" . . . "Not being boy bought-by I am who ox-ward strong on hammering the fire lumber and worth no few-fold rifles is why?"

Pep Club 4.

### Amana Swansdown Peppridge
### "Fridge"

*"There's a divinity that shapes our ends"*
Poise and charm . . . sophisticated . . . cute figure . . . popular with the boys . . . "Gee, I'd *love* to, but . . ." . . . door hugger . . . slim . . . pitches no-hitters . . . "Stop that!" . . . beautiful honey-colored hair . . . does a wicked frug . . . "I *mean* it!" . . . wears latest styles . . . does she or doesn't she? . . . "Look, I'm gonna call a *cop!*" . . . she doesn't . . . "Oh, grow *up!*" . . . dates college guys.

Runner-up, "Miss Teenage Dacron" Contest; Charm Club 2; Future Stewardesses 4.

### Emily May Praeger
"Preggers"

*"Woo'd at haste, wed at leisure"*
Out sick a lot . . . "I must of missed that period!" . . . early morning lav passes . . . cries in Home Ec . . . Emily May is busting out all over . . . excused from gym . . . nothin' says lovin' like somethin' in the oven . . . "Dibs on your pickles?"

Future Homemakers 4; Knitting Club 4.

### Purdy Lee Spackle
"Psycho"

*"He's a rebel . . ."*
Uncontrollable bursts of enthusiasm . . . lots of attention getting qualities . . . actions speak louder than words . . . Angelina Staccato's initials carved in his arm . . . a doer, not a talker . . . often leaves school to take trips downtown . . . waiting for Fungus in the parking lot . . . a man of action . . . Arkansas toad sticker . . . waiting for Zippy in the parking lot . . . arresting personality . . . waiting for Swish in the parking lot . . . moody but well-respected.

Newcomer from Juvenile Work Farm High; Kar Klub 4.

### Gilbert Bunsen Scrabbler
"Univac"

*"The square of the hypotenuse equals the sum of the squares of the adjacent sides"*
Big on trig . . . black lace-ups . . . always prepared . . . lime-green short-sleeve shirts with little notches at the arm . . . slide rule tie clip . . . "Mr. Machine" . . . different color socks . . . takes notes at lunch . . . don't you wish everybody did? . . . "Me sir, I know!" . . . studies in study hall.

Salutatorian; Honor Roll 1,2,3,4; Slipsticks 1,2,3,4; Winner *Time* Magazine Current Events Contest; State Science Fair Honorable Mention; Chess Club 2,3; Stamp Club 1,2; "Math'd Marvels" 1,2,3,4; Radio Club 3,4; Paraboleers 1,2,4; Insect Club 2; Reptile Club 2; Spider Club 1,3; Rocketry Club 1,2,3,4; Grade Average 99.9997; Full 4-Yr. Scholarship, United States War College.

### Faun Laurel Rosenberg
"Weirdo"

*"She marches to a different drummer"*
Free spirit . . . artsy-craftsy-spooky-kooky . . . collects Burl Ives records . . . reads books . . . "You should call them Negroes!" . . . thinks Joan Baez can sing! . . . irons her hair . . . future Freedom Rider . . . black tights and jumpers . . . Peace Corps after college.

Hootenanny Club 4; Arbor Day Committee 3,4; *Leaf & Squib* 1,2,3,4; Drama Club 1,3,4; Pouchinellos 3; Mask & Wig 2,3; Guitar Club 4; Clay Pot Society 3,4; *Kaleidoscope* 2,3,4.

### Maria Teresa Spermatozoa
"Quickie"

*"I never met a man I didn't like"*
It's what's up front that counts . . . low-priced spread . . . "Did you wash your hands?" . . . promise her anything but give her a Pez . . . S.W.A.F. . . . Jayvee Tongue-Wrestling Champ! . . . "Are you *sure* you washed your hands?" . . . P.D.A. . . . good ball handler . . . built like a brick dog house . . . can really do "the jerk!"

Girls' Bowling 2.

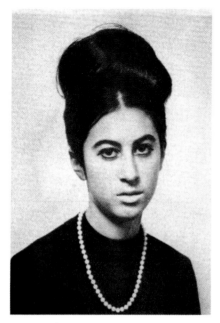

**Angelina Annamaria Staccato**
"Slice"
*"Live fast, die young, leave a beautiful corpse"*
Exotic looks . . . sky-high beehive and three-inch nails . . . wears Psycho's tire chain . . . black net stockings . . . find her at Rollerrama . . . snaps gum . . . all the Bel Aire's singles . . . "Lemme pop it for ya!" . . . eight-inch metal rattail comb . . . roll of nickles in her purse . . . great kidder . . . "Watch it, skag, knock my mascara brush inna sink again an I'll rip every hair outta ya head!"

Future Cosmetologists 2,3.

**Woolworth Van Husen III**
"Lunch Money"
*"Money is the root of all wealth"*
Sharp red Sunbeam Alpine . . . Weejuns . . . "Oh, really . . . ?" . . . smokes Cherry Blend . . . suave to spare . . . Oxford shirts . . . Princeton haircut . . . "Ivy League" clothes . . . Parsons College bound.

Treasurer, Student Council 4; Future Business Leaders 1,2,3,4; Lake Shale Yachting Instructor; Jr. Jr. Jaycees.

*handsome, huh?*

*Hey Larry.
Too bad we never
found out who the
"M.C." (Mad Crapper) was;
I was pretty sure it was
Fungus until even he got one in
his lunchbox! (Gag!) Maybe it was
Swish or Univac? Spag?
Anyway, see ya 'round
this summer . . . if
your mother'll
let ya!
Ha! Ha!
smok
smok!
Wing-
Ding*

**Herbert Leonard Weisenheimer**
"Wing-Ding"
*"Laughter is the best medicine"*
"I'm shakin', I'm shakin' " . . . "Over-shoulder-boulder-holders" . . . "Smok, smok!" . . . a regular Steve Allen . . . knows the real lyrics to *Louie Louie* . . . "She has freckles on her but I love her" . . . "Shake it more than three times and you're playing with it" . . . Chinese Fire Drill . . . "How's yer fern?" . . . favorite subject: lunch . . . "Your mother dives for Roto-Rooter" . . . "I wanna hold your gland" . . . a future writer for *Cracked*.

Tuba Club 2,3, President, 4; Senior Stunt Nite M.C. 4; Audial Visual Aids 1,2,3,4; Canasta Club 1,2.

**Ursula Jean Wattersky**
"Wobbles"
*"I cried because I had no shoes,
and then I met a man who had no feet"*
Good-hearted . . . great personality . . . lots of school spirit . . . a friend to all . . . "A" for effort . . . always puts best foot forward . . . "You'll never walk alone" . . . big help at rummage sale . . . beautiful eyes.

Pep Club 2,3; Floral Clock Club 1; Handicappers for Christ.

**Forrest Lawford Swisher**
"Swish"
*"Blowin' in the wind . . ."*
Theatrical bent . . . sarcastic . . . turtleneck dickeys . . . white socks & sandals . . . crosses legs in class . . . a regular Maynard G. Krebs . . . black socks with white tennis shoes . . . green on Thursdays . . . "digs" "beat" "poetry" . . . quick ma, the Flit!

*Leaf & Squib* 1,2,3, Editor, 4; *Kaleidoscope* 3,4; *Prism* 2,4; Senior Thespians; Drama Club 2,3,4; Pouchinellos 2,3,4; Mask & Wig 3,4; Cloak & Quibblers 1,4; Pen & Ink 3; Cut & Pasters 2; Buck & Wingers 2,3,4; JV Puffbilliards.

Box Baxter, President

Suzi Fitzerman, Secretary

Twinky Croup, Vice-President

Frank Furter, Treasurer

# AFS EXCHANGE STUDENT

Dear Kangaroo School Student and All of Americas,

Now that time is happened for returning of me to my homeland great big happy I say to you I am having been for here to be so long. One question all the time my two ears are hearing for me: "How much am I liking to live this country here?" Always to these my tongue wags, "*Uye lz lz peaüo-h-lštti jhoo jhôo jhoo jhoo jhoo!*" Which means in my people's talking, "How is the one foot to wear of six boots?"

So much all around is difference everywhere. Not so my country. Many houses have each folks here, I beg your for instance. Shiny fast houses with the wheels to live in going back and forthward (such as in the morning time to Kangaroo School and goodnights to pictures which wave in sky outside doors). These shiny houses big as Gurt for sixfold folks family and oxs, but yet not even for sleep except of make-grunting with fresh wives not bought for yet. But that is not three halves of it! Then there is houses of shiny house to live inside with lawn cycle and garden combs only. Then is Giant Gurt of Many Floors with special rooms which are all over. Room for each's own sleeping nights where lay on tables soft like mud. Room to hang up the meat to stink in boxes for making it stink quick as eye folds. Rooms for making earth. And besides plenty of more than that. Then is there even house especial for fur pooch (which they are let to age very old, I make notice of, here, before hung up to stink in your boxes. So much so I'm not seeing one meal full whole of my time here—not so my country!) And then in last place is there House of Kangaroo School where all of each send men sons and daughters still for selling. This is bigger than Leek Palace in Great City of my land! But much fun I get here. Student friends all merry and fine. Always they are making the friendly hello laughter at me. And they have the games with playing such are 52 Pick-Ups and Bet-They-Hit-Softer which do I win always. Or sometime gaming to see for watching. Best of this I like is Throw-the-Lizard. Then there are the room of classes for learning with scratch scratch scratch and so much questions always and harsh talking for good of mine knowing of which favoriteful for me is the room of class where is learning what foods cost in money and then we eat. So is all great good fun. And much the most so of all is little mouths in wall bottoms everywhere. That are when fed the clips-the-paper and other metal meals then belch fire pop! poof!! Ha! Ha! Giant fun! I go now. Bye. Bye.

Ddb̃ Lžmdc Oûaejk

24

**Best Dancers:** Madison A. Jones, Faun Rosenberg

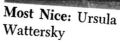
→ *Thinks he is: Larry Kroger!*

**Cleanest Clothes:** Sandra Vort, Gary Gerwin

**Cutest Couple:** Emily May Praeger

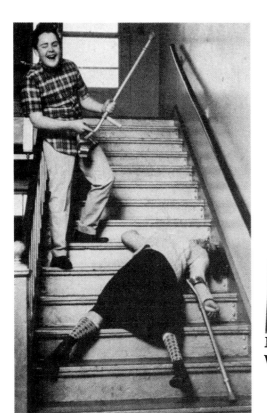

**Most Nice:** Ursula Wattersky

**Class Clowns:** Wing-Ding Weisenheimer, Ursula Wattersky

**Most Likely to Succeed:** Chuck Farley, Suzi Fitzerman

# 1964 Spring Senior Trip

Each spring, a number of seniors and a faculty sponsor break their usual kanga-routines and spend Easter vacation in glamorous globe-hopping! This year, their kanga-route led all the way to New York's well-known Manhattan Island City, New York, when a half-dozen intrepid wallaboys 'n' girls jumped at the chance to be Big Apple bound 'board bouncy buses 'midst Manhattan mirth, magic, and merriment, and plant their perky paws 'round the town as they packed their pouches with a million-and-one-derful marvelous marsupial momentoes!

"It's a small world after all!" peeped plucky peripathetic perambulator H. Leonard Weisenheimer as kanga-runabouts kooled their korn's 'n' kalluses beneath the 1964 World's Fair's unique Unisphere and mulled over a map of konvenient kanga-restrooms!

"Nobody here but just us ignitions!" exclaims teen-space-ager 'n' astro-nut Gilbert Scrabbler as he tickles the business end of a spent but still spectacular NASA space rocketship motor mufler!

"Oooooooh, so *tall*!" kry kowed kanga-rubes as they scan the skyline for the topless tower's terminus and a pack of prankish pigeons (or "feathered rats"), who the spattered sightseers agreed were the foulest of fowls!

"Hey daddy-o, take me to your hipster hootenanny!" giggle "grooving" gadabouts simply mad about meeting their first actual beatnik in Washington Square's wild 'n' wacky "The Greenwich Village."

"Ten points for a wounded wog!" cheer Kefauver good will ambassadorables as "Wing-Ding" wings a washcloth-wrapped weirdo loitering in the United Nations Plaza with the first slingshot hurt 'round the world!

"Okay, you guys, this is a hold-up!" wisecracks a witty Weisenheimer at the very famous Rockefeller Center as he pays tribute to a stocky feller who's *really* got the whole world in his hands!

"Seven...six...five...four...!" ticked off faculty sponsor Mr. Duane Postum as he finished his own "countdown to ten" before aborting the Kefauver Space Program's first attempt to put a marble in orbit from the top of the Empire State Building!

"The eyes have it!" sing-song "honolable kangaloos" as their exciting visit to New York's quaint old Chinatown gives "humble under*glad*uates" a new slant on old ways!

"Now I know why they call it 'flied lice!'" marvels polite midget metropolite Scrabbler at a real Chinese restaurant, although *his* order of the day is an authentic all-American red, white, and blue-plate special!

"Free popcorn, come 'n' get it!" is the kanga-recommendation when boy meets gull on the very famous Staten Island Ferry.

"Give me the Statue of Liberty or give me death!" khorus khaki-faced kanga-rumble-tummies as they encourage their rock 'n' rolling showboat to reach the destination before their delicious Chinese meal reaches its. Sorry to report, our kweasy kanga-retchers forgot to "miss the boat!"

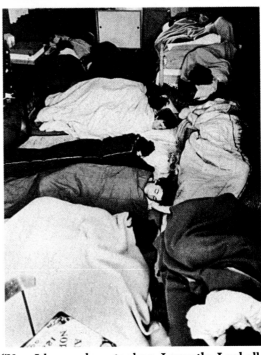

"Now I lay me down to sleep, I pray the Lord all this enjoyable fun and many wonderful educational experiences in my scrapbook to keep!" murmur sleepy kanga-roomies as they kurl up in their kozy kwarters in the very famous and reasonable Penn-Garden Hotel!

27

# Wallababys

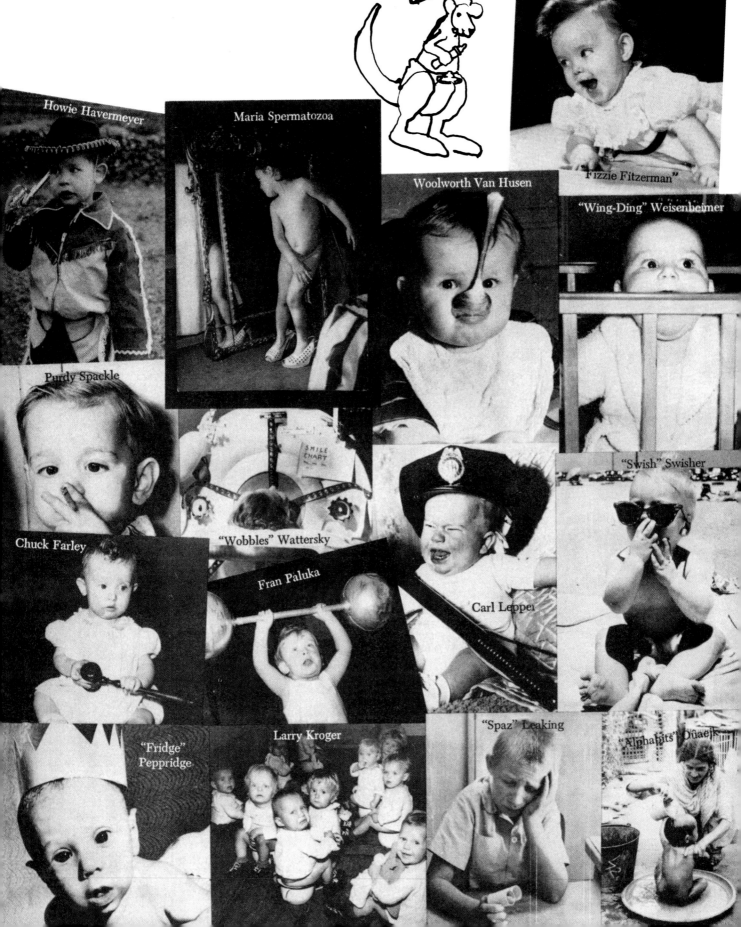

Howie Havermeyer

Maria Spermatozoa

Woolworth Van Husen

Fizzie Fitzerman"

"Wing-Ding" Weisenheimer

Purdy Spackle

SMILE CHART

"Swish" Swisher

Chuck Farley

"Wobbles" Wattersky

Fran Paluka

Carl Leppei

"Fridge" Peppridge

Larry Kroger

"Spaz" Leaking

"Alphabits" Quae

# HISTORY CLASS OF 1964

Four short and fun-filled years ago our forefreshmen brought forth to this high school a new class dedicated to the Principal, teachers, and all the sports teams at C. Estes Kefauver Memorial High. Boy, were we proud to be real teenagers in high school at last. (Of course, our pride turned into confusion every now and then when we got lost in the halls all the time!) And boy, were we happy to find out that Seniors didn't really push your head in the toilets on the first day. (Remember how all those chuckling Sophomores sent us out to get "lunchroom passes" and "left-handed spiral notebooks"?!)

1961: Freedom Riders get killed in Alabama.

That was our Freshman year and we had lots of fun but we worked hard too with difficult academic courses and lots of hard school work. We chose Pinky Albright as Freshman Student Council Representative and Charley Farley for Class President. It was also election year for the rest of the country and Ohio's "native son," Bob Taft, Jr., won a majority of votes in the KHS "Electorial High School," but John F. Kennedy was elected Straw President by default because

1962: Buddhist monk burns to death in Indochina.

Mr. Taft wasn't alive any more. Forrest Swisher wrote the Freshman Class Cheer: "High School, My School, How Do You Do? / We're the New Kangaroos Loyal and True / To the Bright Shiny Orange and the Bold Turquoise Blue / Hop Hop Hop Hop Hop Hop Go Kangaroos!" And in freshman sports our football "Joeys" made a strong showing with a practice loss by only two points to the third team JV Wallabies, though we didn't get to repeat any successes like that in any of the regular league games. As the end of the year rolled by there was the Pep Club Freshman Breakfast Dance. Decorating Committee Chairman Faun Rosenberg selected "There Is No Frigate Like a Book" as the theme

and the entire cafeteria was decorated in cardboard boat cutouts with book covers like *Exodus* and *None Dare Call It Treason* for sails.

Sophomore year went by in a swirl.

As Juniors we were eagerly excited that our Senior year was so close and elected Winky Dempler Class President and Chuck Farley Student Council representative. Everybody had a good laugh when the Buick that practical joking Kar Klub members donated to the Junior Car Smash turned out to be the Principal's and Mr. Conrad was still inside. Ursula Wattersky and Howie Havermeyer took first in city Wheelchair table Tennis and our "Junior Jumper" JV teams added one more win to our sports score. Bruno Grozniak was Dance Committee Chairman for the Junior Varsity Drag and chose "Polka Parade" as the theme. Fizzie Fitzerman was Varsity Drag Queen and Al Orwasecki and his Accordian Orchids played music on this successful occasion. The Junior Class Trip was to Cleveland where we made a special visit to the top of the Terminal Tower Building, thirty-eight stories up! And we could have seen all the way to Sandusky if it had been a clear day!

1963: President Kennedy is assassinated in Dallas.

Junior year ended on a sad note as popular and handicapped Howie Havermeyer went into the hospital and Senior year started on a sad note as he died. And so did President Kennedy. But, as Seniors, we were too full of active pep to stay down long and we bounced right back with a victorious game in our football season and "got the jump" on the St. Vitus Penguins at the beginning of our tournament game with them. Exercising our Democratic institutions in student elections, we made Bob Baxter Senior Class President, Chuck Farley President of Student Council, and Amana Peppridge Homecoming Queen. We went on a Senior Trip to New York, New York, and when we got back "Camelot" was the theme of our Senior Prom. By the time we got finished decorating the gym no one would have known it wasn't a medieval castle in the Middle Ages. Graduation ceremonies were held for the first time ever in the new Mobile Home Bowl Arena Auditorium and everybody agreed that it had been the best Senior Year for the best Senior Class ever at C. Estes Kefauver Memorial High except for the tragic deaths of Howard Havermeyer and President Kennedy and the car accident after the Prom.

KANDID KANGAROOS

Senior BAKE SALE

DETENTION STUDY HALL

It's 1974 and **Vince Lambretta's** a big rock 'n' roll star. He wears his head shaved like the Russian rock groups that are the latest fad do in "Swinging Sevastopol."

**Charles Farley** was just elected to the World House of Representatives as Global Congressman for Greater Dacron.

**Bob Baxter** already helped explore Venus and Mars as an Astronaut in the U.S. Air and Space Force and now he's an Atomic Rocket pilot blasting back and forth between Dacron and New Washington, D.C., for Pan Moon Spacelines.

**Bruno Grozniak** is a Sergeant in the United Nations' Marine Corps, stationed in our fifty-first state—sunny Cuba.

**"Alphabits" Oûaejk** has returned to her native land to found the first chain of drive-in bullockburger stands —McOûaejk's "Over Six Gross Pecks and Many Score Furlongs Sold." And I bet you can guess where all the carhops carry their trays.

**Amana Peppridge** is a big star on three-dimensional smellovision and she's playing the lead role in famous writer **Forrest Swisher's** latest play about Jxlzxt, a beautiful creature from Alpha Centuri, who falls in love with R36m30 from Ursa Major despite the intergalactic war between their two universes and tragically dies in the end.

Also on smellovision all the time are **Winky Dempler, Pinky Albright** and **Twinky Croup,** the Triple-Mint Triplets, singing and dancing a commercial for Triple-Mint, the mentholated fluoride chewing gum that fills tooth cavities and cures cancer.

And fixing those complicated smellovisions is smellovision repairman **Larry Kroger.** But it's no sweat when the set has to go into the shop 'cause all he does is take it off the wall and roll it up.

Famous scientists **Gilbert Scrabbler** and **Belinda Heinke** have won the Nobel prize for inventing a nuclear-powered car that drives itself where you tell it to, a new fungus that cures heart attacks like penicillin, and test tube babies.

But **Carl Lepper** is still waiting for them to invent acne vaccine. Carl is a strontium 90 prospector on Uranus and everybody was glad to give him a going away party.

**Franklin Furter** sells transistorized World Book Computerpedias door to door and they make everybody so smart that **Rufus Leaking** is a Professor of Electronic Medical Math in a Dacron Grade University kinder-garten.

Progress of all kinds has been a big advance for everybody in 1974. Such as **Zippy Jones** is Governor of Mississippi and **Ursula Wattersky** is a Prima Donna in the Dacron Ballet.

**Preggers Praeger** finally found out who gave her tonsillitis. They have a large family and live over a mile up in Trailer Towers, owned by international playboy and Turbo-Yachtsman **Woolworth Van Husen III,** who's married to the famous movie star and sex symbol, Hayley Mills.

**Wing-Ding Weisenheimer** is a top comic in Las Venus where he plays all the big Venusian night clubs—and on Venus the nights are four months long!

**Faun Rosenberg** ran out of things to protest after the World Government fixed up all the international injustice, so she became a famous folk singer singing old folk songs from all the different planets like "Hang Down Your Thorax, Xzyv Vzqqx."

Meanwhile, back at old KHS, **Fran Paluka** has Miss Armbruster's job, except gym courses are all weightless and Fran lets students ride their anti-gravity air-skate wings on the school walks as long as they're careful.

**Fizzie Fitzerman** disappeared back in 1970 and no one knew where she'd gone until Dominic Brocolli took a vacation to Australia and—you guessed it—there she was in the middle of the herd! Hop! Hop! Hop! Hop!

**Underclassmen**

# Junior and Sophomore Homerooms

**Homeroom 104:** Ray D. Aider, Clark Barr, Selma Botti, Terry Daktul, Andrea Dorea, Anita Ficks, Denny Grate, Sal Hepatica, Mason Jarr, Morris Kode, Alice Lost, Jerry Mander, Donna Hannah Mealine, Bill Overdew, Frank O. Prussia, Jason Reignbos, Boris Scilley, Jenny Side, Elmer Sklue, Leah Tard, Sal U. Tory, Claire Voyance, Tupper Weir.

**Homeroom 132:** June Bug, Lafayette S. Cadrille, Katy Didd, Sid Down, Arch N. Emmy, Pat Fanny, Denny Hittme, Gary Indiana, Candy Kain, Ruth Less, Sally Mander, Yetta Nudder, Mel Odios, Rhea Polster, Derry Queen, Rhoda Rhee, Simon Sess, Vic Svaporub, Rhea Tard, Ginny Tonic, X. O. Verrisi, Gale Warnings, Max Welhaus, Bette Wetter, Heather N. Yon, Hans Zoff.

**Homeroom 106:** Trudy Ages, Bob Alou, Anna Baptist, Chris Coe, Holly Cost, Rudy Day, Lynn C. Doyle, Mory Eale, Sally Forth, Doug Grave, Helen Highwater, Gerta Loins, Stu Meet, Chip Monk, Luce Morales, Warren Pease, Vito Powers, Taffy Pull, Amanda B. Reckonwith, Isabelle Ringing, Otto R. Rottic, Ed Settera, Frieda Slaves, Chuck Steaks, Shara Tan, Jill Tedd, Al B. Tross.

**Homeroom 208:** Ann Arbor, Ted D. Baer, Etta Burger, Doris Closed, Bard Dahl, Barry Dellive, Robin Droppings, Io Ewe, May Flye, Alma Gedon, Hy Marks, Holly Hox, Chris Kraft, Ellis I. Land, Penny Loafer, Dell Monte, Baxter Nature, Agatha L. Outtahere, Bunny Pellits, Cheri Pitts, Forrest Ranger, Ron Rico, Cole Shute, Gracie Spoon, May Zola.

**Homeroom 110:** Bess T. Ality, Paul Bearer, Bertha D. Blues, Brad N. Butter, Muriel Cigars, Molly Coddle, Maria Dentist, Eileen Dover, Elaine Down, Herb Evore, Karen Fieding, Annetta Fish, Carmen Ghia, Otto Graph, Clem E. Hans, Cary Hout, Mary Inate, Rex Karrs, Mason Knight, Emmy Nems, Lilac A. Rugg, Cary Scene, Dinah Soar, Walt Step, Anne Teak, Waldo Wall.

**Homeroom 230:** Jerry Atrick, Hy Ball, Jill E. Bean, Kitty Carr, Phil Coe, Stella Constellation, Lee Derhosen, Stan Dupp, Hammond Ecks, Fanny Farmer, Golda Fish, Shirley U. Geste, Lou Gubrious, Beverly Hills, Castor Hoyle, Bella Katt, Al Lergy, Ida Lowers, Pete Moss, Rhoda Mule, Missy Perriad, Carolina Rice, Anna Septic, Cass Tigate, Val Voline, Helen Wheels.

**Homeroom 121:** Sue Age, Peg Board, Poppy Cox, Graham Crackers, T. V. Dinners, Polly Ester, Hope Ferterbest, Cheri Flip, Amber Griss, Tania Hyde, Barbie Kew, Corey L. Layness, Pat Pending, Carol Singers, Phyllis Stein, Mabel Syrup, Jerry Tall, Peg Trousers, Nan Tucket, Bud Vase, Della Ware, Butch Wax.

**Homeroom 236:** Perry Anthrust, Cora Napple, May Balleen, Frank N. Beans, Terry Cloth, Georgia Cracker, Moe Dess, Dinah Floe, Della Gate, Anna Grahm, B. B. Gunn, Anya Honor, Jacquelyn Hyde, Simon Ize, Eddy Kitt, Mandy Lifeboats, Gerta Loins, Lee Mealone, Marsha Mellow, Johnny Mop, Maida Pass, Allen Rench, Sharon Sharalike, Perry Stalsis, Ty Tannic, Tinka Toy, Matt Tress, Val Vita, Lotta Zitts.

**Homeroom 121:** Izzy Able, Hedda A. Borshun, J. L. Breaker, Cilla Cohen, Tab Collar, Joy Anna DeLyte, Buffy Dinner, Matt A. Dorr, Mike Fright, Emmy Grate, Sherry Herring, Bud Hout, Hugh N. Kry, Jimmy D. Locke, Ali Moe, Laureen Norder, Tad Pole, Kurt Remarque, Dick Shunnary, Fay Slift, Cass Stout, Emile Ticket, Barry Tone, Dawson D. Towel, Bess Twishes, Myron Vundergame, Polly Wannakracker, Sadie Word, Buddy Yupp.

**Homeroom 231:** Garrison Belt, Bill Board, Aaron Buoy, Rosa Crucion, Cookie Crumbles, Billie Club, Horace Collar, Hal C. N. Days, Brian E. Diepe, Ben Z. Dreene, May K. Fist, Ali Gator, Philippa Hole, Dixie Kupp, Mark Kards, Daryl Lickt, Taylor Maid, Willy Maikett, Perry Mecium, Roger Overndoute, Sam Pellcase, Everett Reddy, Rod N. Reel, Frank N. Sense, Will U. Shuddup, Eric Shun, Buddy System, Bert Toast, Hal O. Tosis, Milton Yermouth.

**Homeroom 129:** Carter Belt, Dale Lee Bread, Sandy Bunz, Kit Anne Caboodle, Ethel L. Cohall, Dan DeLyon, Io Dine, Ann Dow, Bruce Eazley, Tommy Gunn, Linda Hahnd, Al Ive, Al Ivo, Ava Kashun, Kitty Litter, Mona Lott, Bette A. Million, Bert F. Passage, Collie Raddo, Tommi Rott, Trudy U. School, Vera Similitude, Anne Sodabed, Hardy Tack, Theo Terr, Fran Tickley, Brook Trout, Lee Van der Lurch, Monty Zuma.

**Homeroom 307:** Claire D. Aisle, Barry Berry, Mort R. Board, Lance Boyle, Al O. Bye, Curtiss E. Card, Clara Cill, Idy Clair, Meyer Z. Dhoates, Doe C. Dhoates, Lillian C. D'Ivy, Bud Erdbuns, Chester Fields, Justin Huff, Levi Jaquet, Zelda Karr, Phil Landerer, Bo Linball, Kenny Maikett, Maud O'Lynn, Cliff Pallet, Stu Pendous, George Washington Sleptier, Nick O. Teen, Al Toesaks, Mack Truck, Meg O. Tunn, Neal N. Void.

**Homeroom 137:** N. M. E. Agent, Carson Busses, Earl E. Byrd, Patty Cakes, Derri Anne Connecticut, Moe Dess, Leda Doggslife, Dan Druff, Al Fresco, Ida Hoe, Howie Kisses, Len Lease, Phil Meup, Ira Pent, Ben D. Rules, Ava Sectomy, Sheila Takya, Rose Tattoo, Moe Tell, Les Toil, Lionel Train, N. V. Ubble, Mayflower Van Lines, Chad A. While, Larry Yet.

*2 sweet*
*2 be*
*4 got*
*8*
*Anita*

**Homeroom 309:** Phil Addio, Honor Back, Claude Balls, Gay Barr, Seymour Butts, I. P. Daily, Ima Dork, Ben Dover, Olga Fokyrcelf, Ben Gay, Ava Gina, Peter Guzzinia, Anita Hahnjob, Warren G. Hardon, Jack Hoff, Buster Hymen, Lotta Krap, Anna Lingus, Connie Lingus, Harry P. Ness, Randy Peters, Harry Quim, Joy Ragg, Hugh G. Rection, Red Ruffensor, Hugh Suck, Chastity Suks, Dick Tease, Janet Uppissass, Woody Wannamaker, Dick Wipe, Bette Yeras.

**Homeroom 222:** Penny Ante, Ray Beeze, Barbara Blacksheep, Petey Bowt, Warner Brothers, Mel N. Colic, Petey Cue, B. V. Dease, Benny Fitt, Bette R. Haff, Desi Krashun, Gill D. Lily, Cole Mines, Phil R. Monik, L. O. Quency, Connel Radd, Ben D. Rules, Cleon Sheets, Renata Tampaks, Justin Thyme, Matt Tress, Vic Trola, Al Truist, Aaron Tyres, U. N. Wattarmey, Abe L. N. Willing.

**Homeroom 311:** Marcus Absent, Joan Adog, Claire D. Ayre, Rhonda Campfire, Hose Cannusey, Anne Cestraloam, Flo Dallone, Alfredo D. Darke, Juan Morefore DeRhode, Marco De Stinkshun, Eva Destruction, Alf Fannomega, Juan Formababy, Grace B. Formeels, Pat O. Gonia, Donna History, M. N. Intmann, Pilar Knickersoff, Cole LaDrinque, Viva LaFrance, Alma Life, Bessie May Mucho, Lawrence Nightenjail, Theopholos Punnoval.

# *Freshmen*

*Left to right:* R. Sonn, K. Passo, V. Neck, T. Leaves, C. Señor, C. Spotrunn, G. Purscreepers, O. Very, Q. Gardens, A. Train, U. Nesco, D. Rail, I. Runni, B. Keeney, G. Willikers, X. Zema, O. Tannenbaum, N. Sanity, F. Stopp, X. Sitt, W. Pleasure, W. Funn, T. Totler, P. Ode, E. VanNods, X. Aust, B. Toff, C. Klamp, U. Bolt, I. Beam, D. Tease, I. Dentity, B. Hive, O. Valtine, I. Rate, E. Lann, Z. Roe, S. Enchal, C. Mann, Y. Knot, X. Pert, C. Andski, B. Wildered, E. Late, K. Ration, B. Delumbum, M. Plode, X. Plode, R. D'Vark, A. Kingvoid, A. Cisco, A. Pancho, B. Ginnersluck, D. Frost, B. Hind, D. Cease, D. Cyst, B. Yondapale, D. Day, N. Vinceable, D. Gustibus, C. Sonpass, D. Manrun, E. Valdeeds, A. Lass, I. Dolatry, D. Duest, E. Gerlipz, E. Leventhower, M. Reldail, E. Velli, D. Billatating, N. Fantware, S. Caypartis, E. Ternallov, D. Voutehope, X. Presstrain, L. Bent, E. Titraw, U. Mennature, I. Yoda, I. Hopes, J. Lerr, E. Claire, V. Savvy, B. Aman, T. Doff, B. Bites, L. Efant, A. Cappella, F. Fervessant, D. Kup, Y. Bother, B. Elty, R. Cain, D. Formed, B. Girl, O. Clahoma, J. Hawker, E. Leet, D. Minus, B. Gatt, P. King, A. Hole, O. Leo, G. Mann, E. Nuff, P. Quad, A. Orta, X. Rey, Z. Pitts, T. Schirt, A. Nuss, E. Quator, S. Oteria, E. Rupt, I. Pana, G. String, Q. Tipp, C. Yousoon, M. Ulate, E. Zeoff, A. Winner, D. Troit, E. Zelay, B. Ware, T. Bone, J. Dedd, N. Emma, C. Chanty, O. Fudge, A. Baum, A. Dobie, P. Cann, F. Fort, D. Gennerrett, P. Knutt, X. Lencey, A. Moral, C. Gull, P. Koates, L. Lowe, P. Ness, A. Okey, G. Raff, A. Pendex, C. Sick, C. Note, K. Ryst, Q. Pidd, C. Shell, R. Towne, E. Zeeout, D. Wurst, U. Trau, G. Whiss, N. Doverend, C. Bass, S. Cape, O. Fay, N. D'Vennaira, T. Byrd, N. Chovey, O. Full, O. Kay, D. Licious, T. Kettle, U. Needa, D. Pleat, G. Sass, A. Null, D. Soto, P. Pole, D. Toxin, I. Wash, N. Tropy, J. Walker, I. Dunno, T. Bagg, R. Chury, A. Frame, A. Delweiss, Z. Bra, B. Chermeat, T. Fertue, P. Brain, U. Boat, K. Neincorr, T. Square, E. Sophogus, U. Betcheras, Q. Ball, R. Snick, P. Sanques, U. Turn, C. Breese, B. Stoveburden, Q. Tass, D. Bate, B. Sanbirds, X. Benedict

36

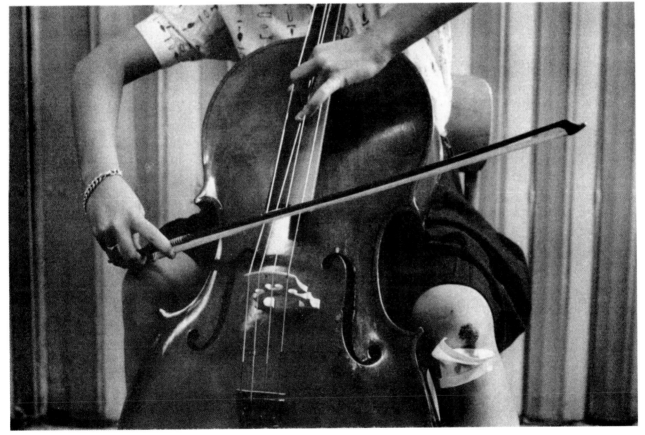

**More Student Freedoms Mean Greater Student Responsibility for Duty to Conscientious Performance of School Obligations**

## Student Council

Student Council achieved many accomplishments during this school year, participating in the decision-making process surrounding numerous conclusions on subjects concerning vital aspects of our daily school lives. One accomplishment which was very fundamental to the functioning of our democratic system upon which America was founded here at KHS was the institution of a Student Suggestion Box. Through this new institution students are now able to place "votes" (suggestions) in their own "ballot box" (the Student Suggestion Box), thereby functioning as the "legislative branch" of a democratic government. Then the Administration can either "sign the bill" (by making a suggestion into a new school rule) or "veto the bill" (by not making a suggestion into a new school rule), thereby functioning as the "administrative branch" of a democratic government. After that, if there is a new school rule to be enforced, the Hall Monitors and Student Court will enforce it, thereby functioning as the "judicial branch" of a democratic government unless the new rule has a Citizenship Demerit Point Penalty of more than sixty demerits because then you get sent to the Dean.

Student Council motto is "Give me liberty or give me death," and members sponsor the annual December Snow Ball whose theme this year was "Winter on Ice."

$$\left( \int_a^b \text{Gilbert Scrabbler } dx \right)^2$$

## National Honor Society

**Honoring Students of the Sciences and Humanities Who Will Go to College Out of State**

National Honor Society emphasizes that it is really an honor to get good grades and the National Honor Society's small copper lapel pin is worn by National Honor Society members much the way that Varsity Sports Team members wear their Varsity Blazers, Varsity Warm- up Jackets, Varsity Sweaters, Varsity Ties, Varsity "K" Letters, JV Letters, Freshman Letters, Special Commendation Patches, Service Stripes, Captain and Co-captain Decorations, and Block K Medallions—to show their proud achievement off to all. For excellent grades are indeed an honor regardless of the esteem in which they are held by the achiever's fellow students. And all the fun and the youthful joy sacrificed to achieve these grades is repaid in full by the excellent grades achieved and the National Honor Society's small copper lapel pin.

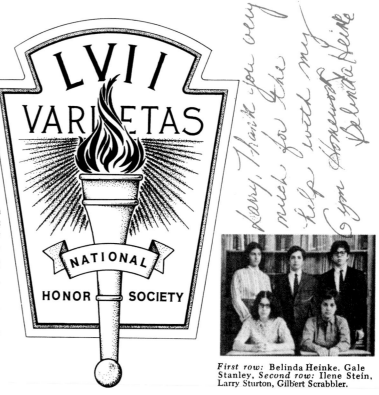

*First row:* Belinda Heinke. Gale Stanley, *Second row:* Ilene Stein, Larry Sturton, Gilbert Scrabbler.

## The Prism

### Kefauver's Newspaper Breaks School Life into Colorful News

Keeping the KHS student body well informed with the facts is the most important principle behind Kefauver's weekly newspaper, *The Prism*, which is run on the principle that a well informed public, which is all of the students in our school, is the most important part of a democracy, which is our school and all its students. Therefore, deciding what can be printed as a fact in *The Prism* is such a big and important job that even Dr. Cornholt takes time out from his busy schedule to help so *The Prism* can serve its important function as part of the democratic system of a well-informed public.

The *Prism* staff writes other things besides facts, though. They also write thoughtful views on important school topics, even those which there are arguments over, so that our newspaper fulfills the double purpose of helping students find out what they ought to be thinking about and what they ought to be thinking about it, too. Plus *The Prism* always has Kefauver sports news because sports are an important part of life and keep us as fit in our bodies as we are in our minds.

### Editorial Staff

Editor in Chief ................................................................Charles Farley
Associate Editor ................................................Herbert Weisenheimer
News Editor ....................................................Woolworth Van Husen
Features Editor ......................................................Wendy Dempler
Sports Editor ..........................................................Franklin Furter
Art Editor ..............................................................Faun Rosenberg
Photography Editor ..............................................Forrest Swisher
Errands Editor ..........................................................Rufus Leaking

### Business Staff

Business Manager .......................................................Carl Lepper
Advertising Manager .........................................Naomi Eggenschwiler

## Leaf and Squib Literary Magazine

### Student Creativity and Originality Is Closely Guided by Helpful Faculty to Promote Good Style and Careful Thinking

*Leaf and Squib* is printed two times a year and is made up of original creative new student poems, writing, and art. Its editors strive hard to emphasize originality, creativity, and newness which they achieve by publishing students' original new creative work. Twice each year, KHS students find it interesting to read stories and verses written by themselves and to see the pictures they drew. This publication is certainly a big plus for new creative talent and original creativity by KHS students whose poems, writing, and art are regularly printed between its covers in the interest of furthering the arts of creativity and originality in new poems, writing, and art by Kefauver students two times a year.

*Pictured left:* Forrest Swisher, *Editor in Chief;* Faun Rosenberg, *Art Editor.*

Lawrence, not goodbye but "adieu" Ciao. Forrest/III

# Kaleidoscope Staff

Editor in Chief Tammy Croup and Business Manager Chuck Farley check complicated deadline schedules while Assistant Editor Suzi Fitzerman goes over the all important "printer's galleys" with Copy Editor Wendy Dempler just as Ad Manager Woolworth Van Husen makes several big last minute sales and Associate Editor Patty Albright runs off some eye-catching publicity releases at the same time that Photography Editor Forrest Swisher snaps one last "pic" and Art Editor Faun Rosenberg prepares her layout tools while Delivery Editor Rufus Leaking rushes in with some much-needed Cokes just before the 1964 *Kaleidoscope* "went to press."

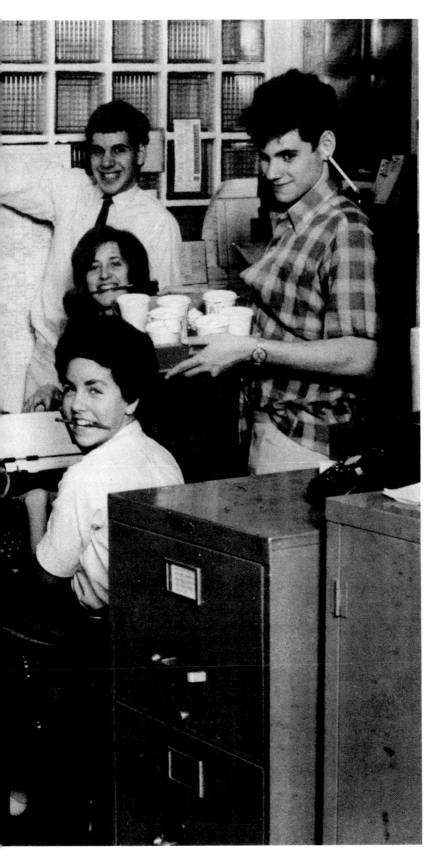

The 1964 *Kaleidoscope* which you are holding in your hands this very minute is the biggest and best *Kaleidoscope* that's ever been turned out at C. Estes Kefauver High. It took lots and lots of hard work to turn out and the *Kaleidoscope* staff did a lot of hard work to do it—designing all the complicated layout designs, drawing all the original and skillful artwork, taking all the difficultly posed and well lighted photographs with the help of Mr. Talmadge from the B.U.T. Studios and developing the film, writing page after page of accurate copy and people's names and typing it all and reading all of it again to make sure everything was spelled right, plus selling ads and copies of the *Kaleidoscope* itself. And that's only a small part of the hard work that this year's dedicated *Kaleidoscope* staff did so well that this year's *Kaleidoscope* is by far the best. Our thanks go out to this year's *Kaleidoscope* staff.

—Staff of the 1964 *Kaleidoscope*

**Tammy Croup**
Editor in Chief

**Suzi Fitzerman**
Assistant Editor

**Patty Albright**
Associate Editor

**Faun Rosenberg**
Art Editor

**Forrest Swisher**
Photography Editor

**Charles Farley**
Business Manager

**Woolworth Van Husen**
Advertising Manager

**Wendy Dempler**
Copy Editor

**Rufus Leaking**
Deliveries Editor

# Mixed Chorus

"Kanga-Crooner's" ever-popular performances were well liked again this year and especially enjoyed was their "Medley of American Melody" program featuring performances of "Hernando's Hideaway," "Buttons and Bows," "Flight of the Bumblebee," "Donkey Serenade," "Kitten on the Keys," and "Theme from Three Coins in the Fountain" which they performed not only in concert at KHS but also in March for the State Republican Roads Commissioners Convention at the Mobile Home Bowl Convention Hall and for the Parkview Lutheran Church's Annual Easter Ode to Song.

*Now more the scrape scrape & as student USAed when born c'no maybe yes?*

# Varsity Club

To further the pursuit of health in mind and body is the aim of the Varsity Club, whose members have all won a Varsity sports letter. But "K-Men" also perform social services and this year they adopted a young girl down on Mill Street and all visited her every Saturday night. Also, they helped decorate the outside of St. Vitus Academy before Homecoming.

*First row:* Bruno Grozniak, Vincent Lambretta. *Second row:* Chuck Farley; Mr. Wormer, *Advisor;* Bob Baxter, *President.*

# Hall Monitors

Hall Monitors are student volunteers who aid all Kefauverites in maintaining quiet passing between classes, tidy lockers, appropriate school dress, and good grooming. Other duties for "Cornholt's Commandos" also including guiding lost freshmen and helping them obtain respect for proper authority.

*Left to right:* Carl Lepper, *Lieutenant-General;* Fran Paluka, *Colonel;* Belinda Heinke, *Captain;* Naomi Eggenschwiler, *Sergeant Major;* Miss Armbruster, *Advisor.*

# Audio-Visual Aids

"Flicker Fellows" are a "reel" boon to education at KHS since they are always on duty to project educational movies in classes or the auditorium. This year they projected the educational movie *Death Takes a Drink in the Driver's Seat* more than two hundred times to Hygiene, Driver's Ed, Family Living, and Boys' Physical Education classes. Also, they plug in school extension cords and adjust the Principal's microphone during assemblies.

*Left to right:* Gilbert Scrabbler, Leonard Weisenheimer, Larry Kroger, Bobby Duvendak, Don Bianco.

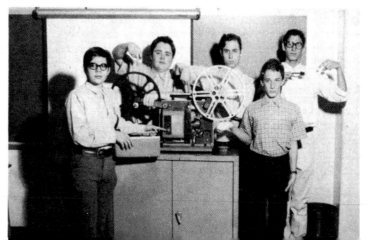

# Junior Achievement

JAers have the best way of learning about American business because Junior Achievement is business capitalism actually at work the way a real corporation, such as these young business people will someday guide and operate, operates. Students form a real corporation, just the way real corporations do, and sell all the shares in it. Then they manufacture something which sells for much more than it costs to make, dissolve the company, and get to keep all the money.

*First row:* Larry Kroger, *Vice-President, Sales and Distribution;* Wendy Dempler, *Treasurer;* Woolworth Van Husen, *President;* Frank Furter, *General Manager;* Bobby Duvendak, *Vice-President, Engineering and Production;* Patty Albright, *Vice-President, Marketing;* Laurie Riggs, *Vice-President, Typing. Second row:* Stephanie Forrest, *Chief of Operations;* Gary Gerwin, *Comptroller;* Charles Farley, *Chairman of the Board.*

# Junior Red Feather

Every year the Jr. Red Cross/Red Feather holds its annual Kefauver Kangaroo Hop of Dimes to collect money for many worthy charities in the Dacron area. This year the theme was "Bounding for Bucks"; however, the campaign was marred by the tragic theft of donated funds being held in the Treasurer's bank account. The KHS senior class pitched in, though, with a Senior Car Smash which cost a quarter for three hits with a sledgehammer so that a donation could be made to the Spinal Meningitis Fresh Air Fund.

*Bounding for Bucks Committee, left to right:* Purdy Spackle, *Treasurer;* Stephanie Forrest, *Homeroom Chairman;* Ursula Wattersky, *Poster Chairman;* Suzi Fitzerman, *General Chairman;* Laurie Riggs, *Typing Chairman.*

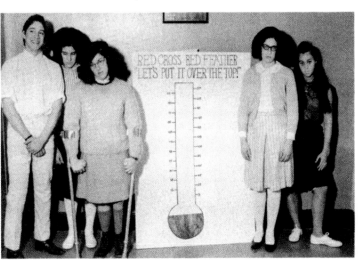

# Kar Klub

Our "Hot Kangarodders" are always showing up in the student parking lot in different brand new car models because a set of hot wheels is the first love of these club members who meet at night to learn everything about late model automobiles and their locks and ignition switches and detachable accessories.

*Left:* Purdy Spackle, *President*

# Pep Club

School Spirit is one of the things which has made America great and Pep Club is the official KHS school spirit organization which leads all the official school cheers at varsity sports games. Honorary president each year is Jumpy the Kangaroo and club activities include memorizing cheers and then cheering them plus lending vim and applause to Citizenship Assemblies, Awards Rallies, the Principal's Speeches, and other school gatherings.

*First row:* Tammy Croup, *Vice-President;* Patty Albright, *Treasurer. Second row:* Frank Furter, Tom Sieler, Kathy Paul; Jumpy the Kangaroo, *President;* Carol Brissie, Peggy Wilder, Lynn Irby, Emily Praeger. *Third row:* Jessica Portmann, Fran Paluka, Robin West, Gary Gerwin. *Fourth row:* Bobby Duvendak, Woolworth Van Husen, Chuck Maypole, Laurie Riggs, Bill Spackle, Larry Sturton, Leonard Weisenheimer.

43

# Future Farmers of America

Kefauveroos and 'Rettes who've got a "green tail" make up the members of the F.F.A. club. Their club project this year was "Our Friend Corn," which won a brown ribbon in the "Best Display on the Theme, 'Green Gold—America's Vegetable Resources'" category at the Silage County Fair Grange Hall.

*Not pictured:* Barry Allstead, Cletus Bartlett, Maud Frank, Leon Hertz, Jerry Luther, Sandra Vort.

# Craft Club

"Crafties" use the school workshop to make all sorts of useful objects in their spare time such as metal knuckle guards for trimming prickly rose gardens, decorative new belt buckle edges, and pistol-grip novelty drinking straws made from old car antennas.

*Left to right:* Tom Sieler, Larry Sturton, Purdy Spackle, Frank Furter.

# Future Stewardesses

Future Stewardesses are career gals on their way up in the world. They meet every Thursday evening to practice friendly grins and balance. The "Flighties" hold an annual "Coffee, Tea, or Milk" for members of the Future Alumni Club and also led this year's Kefauver Safety Kouncil Kampaign, "Seat Belts On and No Smoking in the Student Parking Lot."

*Left to right:* Tammy Croup, Sally Bungart, Amana Peppridge, *Flight Captain.*

# Slide Rule Club

The "Slip Sticks" meet on Tuesdays to learn more about the history, lore, and many handy uses of the slide rule. They compete with the Mathmen from other schools in contests or arithmetic skill and this year Gilbert Scrabbler placed third in the State Divide-Off.

*Left to right:* Tom Sieler, Mr. Ankle; Gilbert Scrabbler, *President;* Belinda Heinke.

# Esperanto Club

Esperanto is a man-made language created to be logical and easy for foreigners to learn. "E-Speakers" hope this modern development will aid in achieving world peace democratically.

*Left to right:* Mrs. Hampster, *Advisor.*

# Wood-Burning Club

The "Board-Broilers" are a hobby club with an interest in an exciting avocation which they use to greatly benefit all KHS students with club projects like the "Jumpy Sez: Are Your Gym Shorts Clean?" signs in the locker room and a beautiful plaque for the Good Stairway Conduct Citizenship Award.

*First row:* Bruno Grozniak, *President;* Bobby Duvendak, Rufus Leaking. *Second row:* Mr. Bohack, *Advisor.*

# Future Optometrists

The eye's have it every Wednesday afternoon after school in room 156 when the "squint squad" takes a peek at a profession that sets its sights for a sharp, clear future and focuses on watchful community service.

*Left to right:* Larry Sturton, Gary Gerwin; Mr. Mannsburden, *Advisor;* Larry Kroger, George Rickley.

# Tuba Club

"Kangaroot-a-toot-toot" is the cheer of the Tuba Club. They're a service organization who give three free concerts each year at the Silage County Old Age Home. And this year they also pitched in to provide the musical accompaniment for the Junior Class Play, "Flower Drum Song," when the school band all had the flu.

*Left to right:* Carl Lepper, Tom Sieler, Leonard Weisenheimer, Gilbert Scrabbler, Betty Rutteldge.

# Future Housewives of America

Homemaking is the oldest profession in the world and KHS F.H.A. members intend to make a lifetime career out of it. Club activities include an annual field trip to the Monroe St. Pick 'n Pay where members learn that nutritious food shopping on a moderate budget is a science just like astrophysics.

*Left to right:* Gale Stanley, *President;* Sally Bungart; Mrs. Butterick, *Advisor.*

45

## Rocketry Club

Rocketry Club members build and explode their own rockets with an eye on the exciting Areo-Space field after college. Their latest experiment, the V-LXXXVI, carried a message from Jumpy to high school students on other planets in outer space. It landed behind the stadium and was retrieved by Coach Wormer.

*Left to right:* Larry Kroger, Gilbert Scrabbler.

## Young People's Society of Tri-Hi Teen Associations

Y.P.S.T.H.T.A. is a city-wide teenage service organization devoted to youth services for Dacron area teens. They're a group on the go with youth on their mind and this year they sponsored the Dacron Teen Council of Young People and hosted the State Youth Conference's Young People's Teen Convention. Y.P.S.T.H.T.A. members also elect regional representatives to the National Young Adult Congress which meets each year in Washington to explore American Young People's role in teenage youth.

*First row:* Bobby Duvendak, Patty Jo Shinski, Peggy Wilder, Sally Pash, Larry Sturton, Gale Stanley. *Second row:* Tom Sieler, *President;* Frank Furter, Larry Kroger, Gilbert Scrabbler, Gary Gerwin, Woolworth Van Husen. *Third row:* Ddb Oûaejk, Pat West, Nancy Ling, Diana Wilkens, Wendy Dempler, Tammy Croup, Sally Bungart, Peggy Riegner, Patty Albright.

## Life Scouts

Being a "lifer" is what Explorer Scouts have in store for them after age sixteen. Life Scouts help teach the many skills of knots, flags, Morse code, and camp cooking to younger Scouts while preparing to be full-fledged Scoutmasters themselves and also having their own Adventure Program which this year included an overnight visit to Indiana, a spring ski-lift trip up Mt. Silo, and a six-mile canoe portage along the Mud River.

*Left to right:* Bob Langlois; Mr. Wormer, *Adviser;* Frank Furter.

## Lincoln Douglas Debating Society

Like the great American debater Lincoln Douglas for whom they are named, the Debating Society members debate important issues with each other for practice and with other schools with an eye towards the state Debating Finals which our "Debate-Makers" didn't make it to this year. But the KHS "Verb-Flingers" did very well city-wide on the topics "Resolved: The United States Should Form a Common Market with Canada," "Resolved: The United States Should Not Sell Wheat to the U.S.S.R. Until Their Communist Government Is Overthrown," and "Resolved: The United States Should Allow Chiang Kai-shek to Recapture Mainland China in order to Avoid Further Shelling of Quemoy and Matsu."

*Left to right:* Charles Farley, *President;* Carl Lepper, *Sergeant-at-Arms. Not pictured:* Gary Gerwin, Belinda Heinke, Faun Rosenberg, Tom Sieler, Forrest Swisher; Woolworth Van Husen, *Vice-President.*

# SociAl Fun

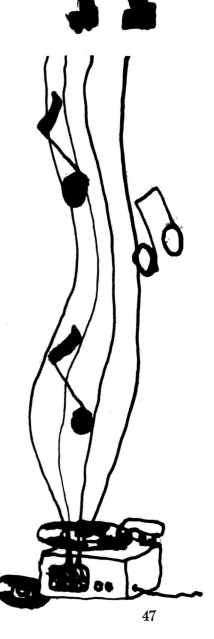

# JULIUS CAESAR

As the lights lowered and the curtain raised with hushed expectancy, a respectably-sized first-night audience of tragedy buffs and surprised *Our Town* fans packed much of the auditorium and sat through the Kanga-roman's three-and-a-half hour drama with an expectant hush.

Kefauver mask-and-wiggers broke a standing 'Fauver footlighter tradition of ten years this fall by presenting the tragically historical *Julius Caesar* by William Shakespeare instead of *Our Town*, a regular faculty favorite. Aided by sets and costumes designed by Miss Mara Schweinfleisch of the KHS Art Department, the histori-cally tragic high school production whisked students and parents alike back to the days of Shakespeare and his ancient Rome of old.

The play, which deals with ambition, politics, friendship, life, death, ghosts, soothsayers, killing yourself, and swordfighting is as true today as it was in Shakespeare's time.

| Cast | |
|------|---|
| Julius Caesar | Forrest Swisher |
| Marcus Antonius | Charles Farley |
| Marcus Brutus | Woolworth Van Husen III |
| Calpurnia (Mrs. Caesar) | Faun Rosenberg |
| Cassius | Lawrence Kroger |
| Caesar's Ghost | Forrest Swisher |
| A Soothsayer | Truman Bradley |
| Polonius | Thomas Sieler |
| Drosophila | Bruno Grozniak |
| Prospero | Suzi Fitzerman |
| Cloaca | Robert Baxter, Jr. |
| Pyramus | Larry Sturton |
| Phosphorus | Gary Gerwin |
| Titus Andronicus | Barry Cantor |
| Citizens of Rome | Charles Farley |
| Author | William Shakespeare |
| Tickets | Wendy Ann Dempler |

*"So shall Rome enslav'd be 'til the cloak of tyranny is brought to its knees!"*—I,i. As Brutus vainly argues with an ambitious Caesar, Cassius (played by Lawrence Kroger) briefly breaks the evening's generally expectant hush as the play comically relieves itself.

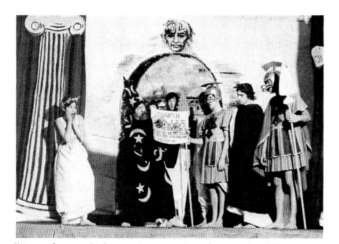

*"A soothsayer bids you beware the Ides of March!"*—I,ii. As Caesar's wife Calpurnia looks on, a warning sooth is said to an unsuperstitious but soon to be dead titled character.

*"Hail Caesar!"* (III,i) cry the conspirators to a wary but nevertheless soon to be dead Julius Caesar who suspects it isn't even raining out, much less hailing.

*"Almighty Caesar, doth thou lie so low?"*—III,i.Here Brutus attempts to pacify an angry and accusing Mark Anthony by telling him that Caesar wouldn't tell the truth about his ambition even if he were not dead.

*"Friends, Romans, countrymen, lend me your ears!"*—III,ii. As Mark Anthony (Charles Farley) speaks to the Roman mobs over Caesar's tragic corpse (Forrest Swisher), the conspirators find that they have been cleverly tricked by Mark Anthony who promised to "bury Caesar, not to praise him" but praises him before he buries him anyway, spoiling the assassination.

*"Great Caesar's ghost!"*—IV,iii. Suddenly in the night, the specter of Brutus' ex-best friend appears and says they "will meet again at Phillipi" where Brutus is going to be defeated. Some think the ghost is real and others tell Brutus the ghost isn't for real. Brutus wonders.

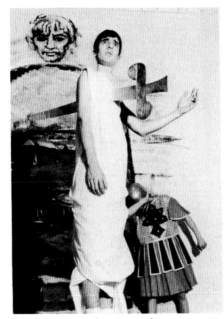

*"To be or not to be, that is the question?"* —V,iv. Brutus, his armies vanquished, already knows the answer to his own question, having convinced his servant to commit suicide on him. Mark Anthony finds his body and calls Brutus "the noblest Roman of them all" which, though dead, too, like Caesar and many others in the play, he would have considered a compliment.

*"Our play is done, t'was sad but fun!"*—Jumpy. As the curtain falls for the final time, the entire cast accepts the many claps and expectant hushes from much of the remaining "friends, Romans, and parents," many of whom stayed on to "lend me your hands" with scenery and general cleanup.

# Senior Stunt Nite '64

"High School Hi-Jinks" was once again the theme for KHS's annual Senior Talent Night held in Moody Memorial Auditorium early this spring. As usual, an unprecedented array of talented 'Roos and 'Rettes amazed classmates, teachers, and proud parents with their consistently unique and singularly varied gifts and abilities.

Hi-Jinks hi-lites over the years have boasted amateur excellence in a wide range of "show biz" arts including pop tune pantomimes, humorous monologues from literature, precision cheering, calisthenics to music, a cappella humming groups, show-stopping kick-lines (with suspiciously hairy legs!), rhythm bands, interesting collections, realistic first aid dramatizations, colorful slide shows, crack acrobatic marching teams, yodels around the world, simulated underwater ballets, wax comb orchestras, balloon sculptures while-you-wait, "soft shoe" dance routines, whistling, rangements of the Pledge of Allegiance, choral arsimultaneous pig latin translations against time, making faces, flash cards, and girls' beanbag throwing exhibitions.

"There's no business like show business," goes the old saying, and after this year's spotlight spectacular everyone agreed that the class of '64 showed they too had no business in show business like nobody's business.

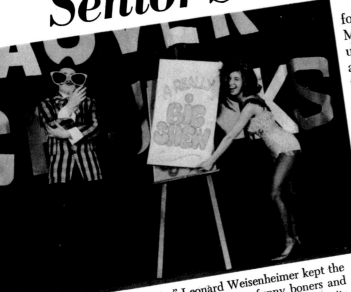

"Gagster of ceremonies" Leonard Weisenheimer kept the ball rolling in the aisles with rib-tickling funny boners and his million-and-one identifiable impressions of our favorite comedian.

Honorably mentioned second Fourth Place runner-up Frank Furter made the audience say "oo" and ah" with magical feats including sawing a board in half, changing ice into water, untying big knots, and making a marshmallow disappear from his mouth.

Ursula Wattersky tapped and tinkled her way to a seven kt. gold-filled Admirable Effort Award for her well-received waterglass interpretations of "Papa Hayden's Dead and Gone," "Holiday for Waterglasses," and "You'll Never Walk Alone."

Students were given an exotic taste of "way out" entertainment as they were treated to Faun Rosenberg's and Forrest Swisher's authentic bohemian song-readings of "Greenleaves," "Hang Down Your Head, Tom Dooley," and the first portion of "Michael Rode the Boat Ashore Alleluia."

Carl Lepper's remarkable "Uncle Carl and Mr. Laffy" proved he was "no dummy" when it came to pulling the wool over our ears by throwing his voice while eating a candy cigarette and making Mr. Laffy "sing" without moving its lips.

"Look ma, no insurance!" Gary Gerwin might well have good-naturedly quipped as he nailed down the Silver Consolation Certificate for Above Average Excellence and raced to make a five-minute guest appearance at Dacron City Hospital for a minor splinter removal.

A sure winner of the Girl's Co-ordination Medal had her hopes dampened when state fire regulations threw cold water on "Patty Jo and her Flaming Baton."

Students were given an exotic taste of entertainment from other lands as they were treated to an authentic native "foot dance" by KHS's A-OK AFS Exchange Kanga-romper Ddb Oûaejk who brought down the house and half the stage to share a Silver Certificate and an ambulance with senior Gary Gerwin.

Kudos for Komical Kanga-kut-ups went to four Liverpool look-alikes and their "wiggy" rendition of "She Loves You Yeah Yeah Yeah." Too bad the "Mercy sound" didn't apply to eardrums!

Musically-minded seniors Lambretta and Scrabbler performed a toe-tapping duet which while failing to win a prize earned them a special Judges' Exemption from the traditional Grand Finale of Encores.

Kulture-konscious Kanga-kon-noisseurs packed away a pouchful of pleasure as prima balleroona Naomi Eggenschwiler stunned the Judges with her classical interpretation of the hatching scene from "Swan Lake."

"Encore! Encore!" the entire audience might well have shouted as it was brought to its feet and given directions to cloakrooms and exits amid thoughts of "Bravo!" and stretching and coat-finding. Once again, a whole-hearted Kangaroo klass had proved the old adage that "talent at Kefauver Memorial High is 1 percent inspiration and 99 percent respiration!"

51

# Home Coming

Football jerseys were dampened but our spirits remained high 'n' dry when an unexpectedly heavy thundershower drove KHS's annual half time ceremonies indoors to Moody Memorial Gym. There, the traditional "Parade of the Cars" around the field was replaced with an equally exhilarating "March of the Students" around the very lovely Homecoming Queen Amana Peppridge seated on her "Folding Chair of Honor," giving us an even closer look and a fine opportunity to dry off before the second half.

As luck would have it, the second half was delayed because the new 1964 Ford convertibles kindly donated for the occasion by Grabski Motors had filled with water by then and sunk wheel-deep into the mud, but waiting for the towtruck only gave students, parents, and old alums a chance to enjoy more hot cider and cold donuts in Moody Memorial Gym.

Although the ensuing moral victory against St. Vitus was offset by the Kefauver bleachers' sinking into the mud and the tragedy of President Kennedy's tragic death, Homecoming '64 was an occasion for students, parents, and grads to come together in the same gym at the same time and look at each other out of the rain.

That evening, before the Homecoming Dance began, Kefauver students offered a moment of kanga-remembrance for a late, great President. Following the minute of kanga-respectful silence, Senior solemnity gave way to kanga-rollicking as we plunged into the fun and refreshments with the same spirit that JFK dove into the water after his P.T. boat was heroically sunk.

Homecoming festivities commenced when Queen Amana Peppridge was officially crowned by runner-up Tammy Ann Croup, who lost the coveted title by a slim 313–314 margin which by a remarkable coincidence was the same as the number of girls vs. boys in the school!

While unseasonable weather rolled out the mud carpet outside, inside Queen and Court accepted the homage and balloons of damp but undaunted subjects whose wet clothes only brought enthusiasm to a "Kefever" pitch!

As a further mark of respect, we twisted our grief away with "vigah" as He would have wanted us to to the rhythm of the popular "P.T. 109" song, which under the circumstances had an even deeper significance as well as its usual delightful dancebility.

Dear Harry,
It's been loads of fun knowing you (there're forget sixth period Study hall!) I think you're a super person and I'm really sorry about Twinky (Eggy is a wonderful human being, too...heh, heh!) See you this summer when you come over to mow our lawn...
Hugs,
★ Amana

52

Senior Prom "CAMELOT"

Will you?

Love to!

1
My gown I'll wear with style and flair!

4
Give your socks pep with a box step!

2
Blooms for the prom? Your mums and her mom!

5
Party and fun 'til quarter to one!

3
Prince Charming states, "Your carriage awaits!"

6
Mighty late but what a date!

# PROM "IN-FORMALS" A NIGHT of KNIGHTS

"Camelot's" great decorations make a "grand" entrance for Orange-and-Bluebloods!

When it comes to refreshments, our Kanga-royalty "bunnyhops to it!"

Chaperones Mr. Mannsburden and Mrs. Fitzerman's annual Charleston made Camelot'ers glad they came a lot!

A lady-in-waiting for a knight to remember!

Greetings, miladies, I'm Alan Funt and . . .

A certain Sir Dancelot catapulted kangaroos' spirits to record highs!

If her Highness' shoe fits, drink it!

*I was hardly drunk at all. I was just kidding!*

Looks like an "earl"-y "knight" for a certain basketball "court jester!"

A sly knave makes a cutting remark!

Mr. Mannsburden climbs on a para-pet-ers!

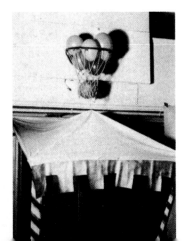

# Dances by the Dozen

"Beatnik Nite" let KHS kats 'n' kittens "get hep" to a taste of bohemian non-conformity as sandaled kanga-rebels-without-a-cause got "hopped-up" on cool jazz and hot dogs. First prize for best "way-outfit" went to Suzi Fitzerman, '64, who "made the scene" in a turtleneck sweater (natch!), "shades," a pair of old "clamdiggers," and a "frantic" madras bandana!

Weekly "sock-hops" kept kanga-restlessness down to a minimum as Kefauverites cavorted to their Kefavorite kanga-recordings while Miss Armbruster gave generously of her valuable time to keep our feetless footwear from getting all mixed up or lonely.

Early October's "Sadie Hawkins Day" dance magically transformed our bouquet of wallflowers, shrinking violets, primroses, and snapdragons into vivacious Venus flytraps, much to the delight of every KHS narcissus and pansy.

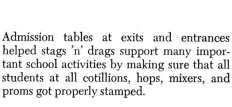

Admission tables at exits and entrances helped stags 'n' drags support many important school activities by making sure that all students at all cotillions, hops, mixers, and proms got properly stamped.

Young Men's Christian Association "Teen" dances let kanga-representatives of our school meet other students from the community and help cut mutual problems down to size by flattening out new roads to understanding.

57

# Varsity Football

## 1963 Kangaroo Pigskinners "Bound" for Victory

And a big victory it was when in the last seconds of only the season's sixth game QB "Flinch" Baxter faded back for a pass to find 'Roo receiver "Zippy" Jones checked 20 yards upstream into hometown territory. Clutching the leather ovoid to his sweat-drenched jersey, "Flinch" flicked his eyes and ran for daylight but, blocked by Prendergast tackle "Lump" Zumpsky, spun on his spikes and lammed it for the Lamprey uprights instead. While Kefauver linemen's famed "turquoise wave" beat it towards the bleachers on every side, Baxter bobbed and weaved down the long nine yards to goalpost glory, only to almost flub the fabulous when, just after a neat side-step swivel as Lamp guard "Mountain" Mojek slipped on a paper drinking cup, "Flinch" was tackled from behind on the TD threshold, barely managing to pound the pigskin into Prendergast pay dirt for a six point payoff and a hard won win.

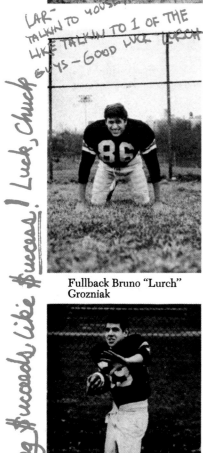

*LAR- TALKIN TO YOUSE ALWAYS BEEN LIKE TALKIN TO 1 OF THE GUYS - GOOD LUCK LARCH*

*Larry, NOthing succeeds like $uccess! Luck, Chuck*

Fullback Bruno "Lurch" Grozniak

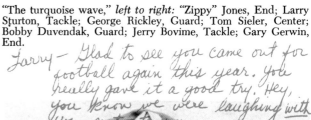

Quarterback Bob "Flinch" Baxter

"The turquoise wave," *left to right:* "Zippy" Jones, End; Larry Sturton, Tackle; George Rickley, Guard; Tom Sieler, Center; Bobby Duvendak, Guard; Jerry Bovime, Tackle; Gary Gerwin, End.

*Larry— Glad to see you came out for football again this year. You really gave it a good try. Hey, you know we were laughing with you, not at you — Bax*

Coach Vernon Wormer

Halfback Charles "Chuck" Farley

Halfback Vincent "French" Lambretta

Season's finish, however, was a return to the pace set in opening games with valiant K-Men efforts falling short against repeated ball hoarding by score-happy opponents for a final scorecard of one win, eight losses for Kangaroo's Galloping Gridiron Grinders.

| | | |
|---|---|---|
| Kefauver ............0 | Silage Rural Consolidated ..........18 |
| Kefauver ............0 | Benson Bobcats ..........................21 |
| Kefauver ............0 | St. Vitus Penguins ......................27 |
| Kefauver ............2 | Tucker Wingnuts ........................36 |
| Kefauver ............0 | Tiffin Edsel Ford ........................16 |
| Kefauver ............6 | Prendergast Lampreys ..............0 |
| Kefauver ............0 | Harding Hyenas ..........................48 |
| Kefauver ............0 | Arnold Turncoats ......................37 |
| Kefauver ............0 | Akron Dewey ............................24 |

Unlucky fumble gave forty-eight-point lead to Harding Hyenas.

Well-planned Kangaroo defensive ball play held Tucker Wingnuts to thirty-six points.

Quarterback "Flinch" Baxter charges into the end zone for a winning TD against the Prendergast Lampreys.

Team Doctor Morey Horowitz took time out from private practice to be ready by his office phone during every KHS home game.

New plays and a well-practiced quarterback sneak failed to avail against St. Vitus Penguins.

Sorry, Jumpy, that'll cost you fifteen yards!

59

*KHS season stamina brought student cheers as "yard-chargers" fielded full team for every game!*

*Ramblin' 'Roos impressed whole school with several first downs in '63!*

*"Tackle-Takers" hopped to high safety score with no fatal in-game injuries!*

# Basketball
## Jumpster Jump Stars "Leap" into Lead at '63–'64 Season End

Kefauver Frontline Five, *left to right:* Charles Farley, Bruno Grozniak; Mr. Duane Postum, *Coach;* Vince Lambretta, Box Baxter, Madison Jones.

'Roo Rafter-Grazers faced tough competition in this year's Greater Dacron League.

KHS was out in force for the prestigious post-season exhibition tournament in the Mobile Home Bowl Arena and right from the tip-off it was excitement galore for 'Roo rooting ranks as varsity Roundballers chalked up their first leading score of the year—a two-point jump on St.Vitus, which kept the Vite Five's score locked in the ought slot for more than a minute before the Web-Foot Swish-Wizards lobbed one in to level out the lay-up ledger.

Overall, it was a tough season for our board bouncing Bucketeers but their play was as tough as the defeats they had to face—as was shown by the moment's-long shut-out of St. Vitus in Home Bowl display play even though Peng Parquet-Tippers finally managed a twenty-two-point first quarter comeback.

Coach Postum puts plenty of confidence on our Set-Shooters' growing skills since this year's all-senior slate is a safe bet for basket betterment in next season's play. And sure shooting, such as 'Roo Soft Shoes showed at the beginning of their big tourney vie with St. Vitus, goes to agree plenty with Coach Postum's predictions.

| Us | Them | |
|---|---|---|
| Kefauver ........20 | Benedict Arnold ................................. | 96 |
| Kefauver ........21 | St. Vitus ........................................... | 81 |
| Kefauver ........16 | Warren Harding ............................... | 92 |
| Kefauver ........12 | Boss Prendergast .............................. | 79 |
| Kefauver ........15 | St. Vitus ........................................... | 85 |
| Kefauver ........20 | Tucker Technical ............................. | 90 |
| Kefauver ........ 7 | Dayton George Washington Carver ..116 | |
| Kefauver ........19 | Ezra Taft Benson ............................. | 76 |
| Kefauver ........23 | Benedict Arnold ............................... | 86 |
| Kefauver ........18 | Boss Prendergast .............................. | 89 |
| Kefauver ........17 | Warren Harding ............................... | 68 |
| Kefauver ........19 | Middletown John Foster Dulles ........ | 77 |
| Kefauver ........10 | Ezra Taft Benson ............................. | 93 |
| Kefauver ........11 | Tucker Technical ............................. | 91 |
| TOURNAMENT | | |
| Kefauver ........17 | St. Vitus ........................................... | 73 |
| Kefauver ........20 | Tucker Technical ............................. | 96 |

## "Nice Try" Was the Hallmark of Kangaroo Hoop Hopper's Varsity Basketball Play as Winless Season Stalled Dribble Demons' Victory Drive

# Wrestling

Many were the hard fought victories won by 'Roo Rasslers during last winter's action. No more had the season opened than success came the way of Grappler Hondo Vogel in a fight for life with massive internal hemorrhaging. Then K. High's "Hammer-Locker" Chip Eldridge triumphed in a dramatic struggle to regain the use of his right arm. Richard Wanzer won at a walk when he fought a pitched battle with disabling spinal contusions, and Tom Sieler licked a tricky and dangerous spleen rupture in the final period of his hospitalization. Wrapping up the season, ninety-seven-pounder Larry Sturton put a real Full Nelson on the dizzying effects of his three grave skull concussions, while prospects look bright for Eddie Decker, who should be out of Dacron General by August.

*Left to right:* Bob Baxter, 154 Weight Class; Vince Lambretta, 175; Bruno Grozniak, 165; Charles Farley, 145; Coach Vernon Wormer. *Camera shy:* Larry Sturton, 97; Chip Eldridge, 103; Eddie Decker, 118; Richard Wanzer, 127; Tom Sieler, 138; Hondo Vogel, Heavyweight.

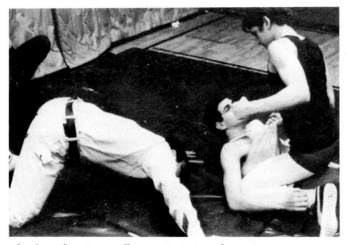

Chuck Farley staves off near pin in Prendergast meet.

Harding mat-man's footwork puts 'Roo Rumbler Chip Eldridge off balance.

## "Mat-Backs" Cast for a Loss as Bad Breaks Crippled Last Leg in KHS Waltz to Winner's Circle

Vince Lambretta has an eye out for chance to topple Tucker Tech contender.

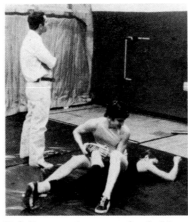

Bob Baxter tries a new leg hold on Benson Bobcat opponent.

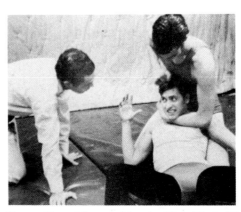

Bruno Grozniak uses his vise-like chin hold to turn tide in St. Vitus Match.

# Track and Field
## "Lane-Burners" Not Beaten by Any Opponent

A trackman's real competition is always with himself, so no one can say that anybody else beat our "sharp-shoes" in '64 even if the KHS "Kangarunners" hotly contested constant striving with their own abilities and courage was occasionally marred by losing all the time in every meet for this popular sport whose most popular event by far was the pole vault. Which was certainly our big school crowd pleaser because they don't call us Kangaroos for nothing and the eight-foot threshold was no barrier to Kefauver "leap-leggers" especially with the new fiberglass poles which somebody got mixed-up about with Coach Postum's fly rod during practice and Mr. Postum's brand new Shakespeare reel got caught in the high tension wires and the gas and electric company had to come and get it down with a hydraulic ladder truck which accidentally short-circuited all the electricity in the cafeteria refrigerators and the tuna steaks spoiled and everybody had to be allowed to go eat lunch at Burger Heaven the next day.

*First row:* Carl Lepper, Purdy Spackle, Madison Jones, Richard Wilder. *Second row:* Vince Lambretta, Bruno Grozniak, Bob Baxter, Tom Sieler, Lester Hadad, Herbert Weisenheimer, Don Sharp, Larry Kroger, Chuck Farley; Frank Furter, *Manager;* Mr. Postum, *Coach.*

Shoelaces were often a "glass heel" for our "Cinderfellas"; here Larry Kroger makes a "pit stop" in 440 against Ezra Taft Benson.

The one win in an event we did have was our biggest, though; "Zippy" Jones ran the mile in 4:11 at an out-of-state meet with the Confederate Dixie Rebels from Jefferson Davis High in Lynchburg, Tenn.

*KHS "Spike-Heels" help Kefauver gain "Best Sports in the City" title with polite congratulations they extended to every Greater Dacron area team.*

# Swimming *Competition in Water Logged New Records*

*First row:* Ned Tuckerworth, *Coach;* Jerry Ollier, Nelson "Shrimp" Scampoli, Gregg Pietras. *Second row:* Walt Osborne, Chuck Farley, Bruno Grozniak, Rufus Leaking. *Third row:* Don Ellis, Bill Grange, Randy Wertz, Bob Baxter, Jim Zollinger.

In their first year of unparalleled performance, another new KHS athletic squad broke all its own records in the space of only six months. And that was the big payoff for a team which was determined to succeed—even against itself.

The whole summer, backyard wading pools all over the Kefauver school district resounded with the cries "Stroke left, breathe right, blow out, kick! Stroke right, breathe left, blow out, kick!" Until by September, team captain Bob Baxter was ready to set a 1:54 school record for fifty-yard free-style which he swam sidestroke hot on the tail of cramp-plagued Hyena "Pool-Paddler' Mark Bowin in our first league match with Warren G. Harding. Bob was far from done, though, and came back to break his own school record with a 1:18 time and Chuck Farley's backstroke and butterfly records with times of 1:04 and 2:11 while managing at the same time to also place third in the individual two hundred yard medley against Prendergast after disqualification of both Lamprey "Fluid-Floggers."

But success over each other was only part of our "Wave-Makers'" story of '64, since they also fought a long, grueling season to get the team in shape against not only Greater Dacron schools but also in nonleague meets with Y Minnow and Tunafish Classes, the Golden Ager Angel Fish, Boys' Club Jr. Deep-End Division, and others.

### Splish Splash
### New 'Roo Sports Squad Takes A Bath As KHS Athletic Department "Jumped" Into "Finny Fray"

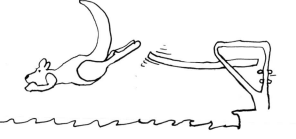

66

# Bowling

## Kangarollers "Pin Down" City Kegler Krown

*Just call me "King Pin"!!*

Top Jock Team triumph in 'Roo Sports Spotlight for '64 went to KHS undefeated Alley Aces who "launched the lumber" for sixteen straight lossless lane leads and rolled into first place with "room to spare."

The Gutter-Cheater's vise grip on victory catches kudos for Coach Armbruster, who kept our Split-Lickers "out on strike" with a 546 team total alley tally average!

*Front row:* "Wing-Ding" Weisenheimer. *Back row:* Miss Armbruster, *Coach;* "DOM" Brocolli with greater Dacron League Championship Bowling Trophy; "Spaz" Leaking.

# Gymnastics

Jumpy had something new to jump up and down about this year when KHS floored its first Gymnastics team—and it was a big first in more ways than one as Kefauver became Greater Dacron's only school to "sport" a squad for this exciting athletic activity.

The tightly attired Horse Hoppers' record went unblemished in their premiere season with nine defaults and a strong showing against Senior Girls' Tumbling in Intramural scrimmage.

*First row:* Barry Cantor, Bob Baxter, Chuck Farley. *Second row:* Bruno Grozniak, Truman Bradley. *Third row:* Mr. Sneedler, *Coach.*

## Jumper Gymmats Reign Unchallenged, Ring Swingers in a League of Their Own

# C. Estes Kefauver Memorial High Marching Band

Led by the very capable Mr. Dwight Mannsburden, the C.E.K.M.M.B. kanga-root-ta-too-tooters and -tummers are always on hand to help take our minds off the game and the Esterettes.

"Music hath charms to soothe the savage beast," and Mr. Mannsburden does just that by backing the football team with kanga-rousing field programs including intricate band formations which if Kefauver fans were in helicopters or Goodyear blimps would very likely spell out many fine words of encouragement such as *beat, win,* and *go,* the last word often with an exclamation mark!

This season's program also contained many "theme" numbers, the most popular of which, "Chattanooga Choo-choo," had the entire band form a locomotive with a smoking stack!

KHS regrets the indefinite loss of Mr. Mannsburden's services for next year due to injuries suffered when a smudge pot exploded in Mr. Mannsburden's hat.

## C. Esterettes

Our group had 47 percent lower gravity!

C. Estes Kefauver High was fortunate once again this year to have the help of Mr. Milton Diller in organizing the Esterettes. A crack team of undergraduate precision acrobatic marching twirlers, the Esterettes furnish dazzling exhibitions of simultaneous baton magic during half times, time outs, and other exciting lulls in KHS athletic programs.

Mr. Diller, who kindly donates time from his regular duties as V.F.W. Community Affairs Council Field Representative Coordinator, gives Esterettes much enjoyable discipline and a healthful head start in the half time program of Life.

Split-second coordination plus snug costumes helped pack them in at KHS sporting events.

"On our toes, girls!" encourages "Killer" Diller as he lends his high-steppers a helping hand to give them a leg up on putting their best feet forward.

# Girls Sports

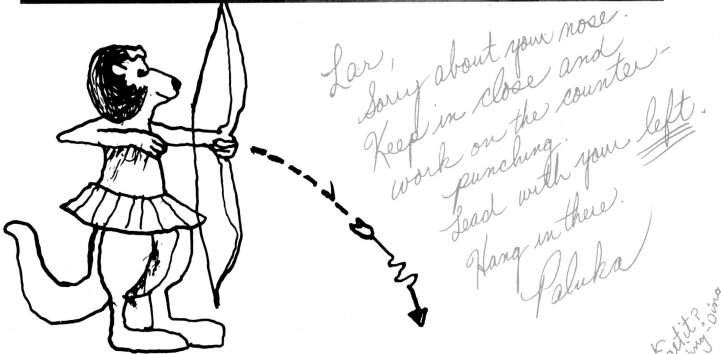

Lar,
Sorry about your nose.
Keep in close and
work on the counter-
punching.
Lead with your _left_.
Hang in there.
Paluka

K, get it? diving-diving

Teaching Girls' Physical Education at KHS is Miss Marilyn Armbruster. She has taught us all plenty about how important the art of physical exercise is to health, fitness, and "fighting flab" because girls have muscles but are often not told about them when they are young. She is always checking our bodies to examine progress we have made in various places toward achieving the robust firmness, strong arches, and healthful stance which she teaches us are so important to vigorous and vimful well-being.

Miss Armbruster works hard at teaching Physical Education. She is always on the job holding our feet while we try a hand stand, grasping us firmly by the ankles as we learn a swim stroke, or just helpfully adjusting an untied gym shoe. Thanks go to Miss Armbruster for our physical education in pep and posture which will aid us in any walk of life whether we become wives and mothers or work first.

**Aqua-Hockey,** played with swim fins, a weather balloon, and field hockey sticks in the shallow end of the school pool, is a perennial favorite. This year's undefeated "Blue Caps" intramural team captained by Fran Paluka played our KHS faculty members in a benefit game for the Deaf Folks Home. Blues were leading by six when Mr. Sneedler got caught in the filter grate and Coach Wormer had to give him artificial respiration through a garden hose until the Fire Department could drain the pool.

**Tumbling** teaches skill, dexterity, and muscular coordination that you'll need to learn the arduous sport of tumbling which has all the grace and beauty of the dance without any of the music. Here, Fizzie Fitzerman exhibits the difficult Arc de Triomphe position which resulted in a painful cramp for even such a skilled gymnastette as Fizzie whose father had to borrow a pickup truck from the Shell station to take her home because the Nurse and Miss Armbruster couldn't get her through the school bus door.

There's plenty of good health in **badminton,** and our "Grey Shirts" intramural team practicing *, right,* got all of it in a marathon match with WOIO "Nice Guys" disc jockeys to raise money for a new Kangaroo suit after Suzi Fitzerman's boyfriend had an accident in the pouch on the way home from the King of Hearts Dance. "Grey Shirts," led by Captain Fran Paluka, won 7,650 to 315.

Talk about fun? Well, that's what **volleyball** is in a nutshell, especially when Captain Fran Paluka is serving for the "Green Shorts" team. They won every game this year except for the one where Fran was penalized for the serve she bounced off a girder in the gym ceiling that hit the back wall and then smashed into opposing player Belinda Heinke, breaking her glasses and dislocating her shoulder.

70

# Cheerleaders

### *"Jump up, pop up, leap up, bounce. Hop, skip, spring, bound, vault, buck, pounce!"*

The KHS Kangarooters lead the rooting for our Kangaroos, and they lend some "good cheer" to our whole school with their spirited chanting and loud yells. The Kangarooters' motto is "Alma Mater," and before every football game they lead the entire student body that came in a chorus of the Kefauver School Anthem while everybody faces the kangaroo-shaped weather vane on the cupola over the west hall south door:

*Larry,*
*To a really swell guy! It really sure was a shame that you and the Twink never got together. She was really close to her aunt and really thought she'd have to go to the funeral on prom night.*
*Luv ya,*
*Pinky*

### Kefauver of Thee

Kefauver of thee
Sing out we for e'er.
Far from us can flee
Thy sweet memory ne'er.
May our Father, stern 'fender
Of thy Founder's bright aim,
Aye excite thee, firm mentor
Alma Mater, with Fame.
And may Knowledge inflame
E'en study and game.
Hallowed be thy name:
Kefauver.

Varsity Kangarooters, *right to left:* Pinky Albright, Twinky Croup, Amana Peppridge, Winky Dempler.

Cheering tryouts are always an important event every year. Here, would-be "Shrill Shouters" holler the KHS Fight Cheer:

Hey, Team, forget that fumble!
Don't you let your spirits tumble!
Don't you grumble!
Don't be humble!
We lost the game,
But we'll win the rumble!

*Larry—*
*To a really swell guy! Really sorry about that prom mix-up. Twink was really sick that afternoon— she must've thrown up a zillion times! Luv ya— Winky*

Stand up!
Sit down!
Squat on your seat!
Lay on your back and wiggle your feet!
Hop on one foot!
Hop on two!
Who are we for?
KANG-GA-ROO!!

Interference!
Clipping!
Referee's blind!
We're not losing,
We're just behind!!

Backfield in motion!
Score's a mistake!
Give 'em a penalty!
Give us a break!

Punt!
Punt!
Punt, punt, punt.
Kangaroos, Kangaroos,
Kick it toward the front!

# DOWN Memory Lane

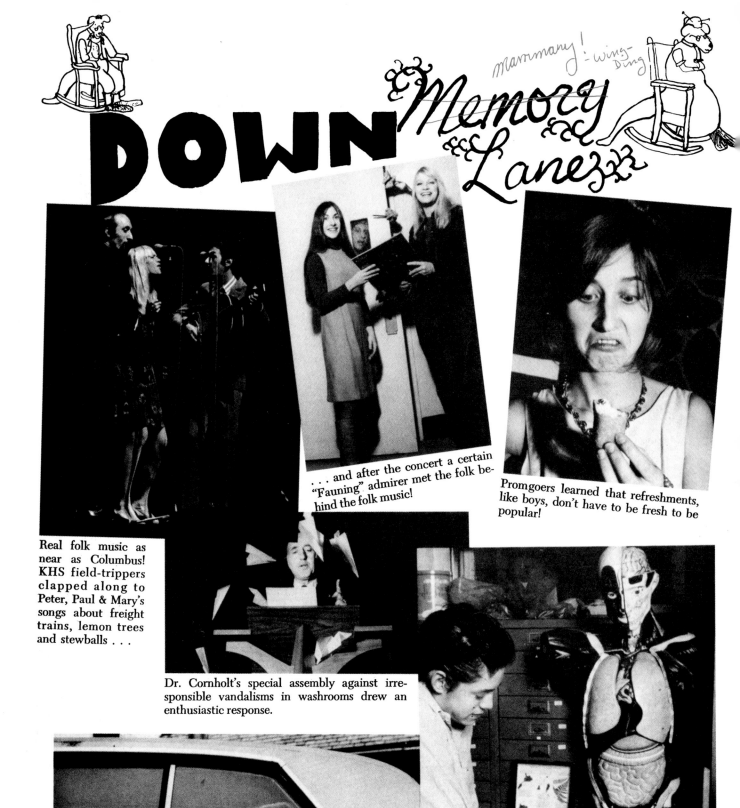

... and after the concert a certain "Fauning" admirer met the folk behind the folk music!

Promgoers learned that refreshments, like boys, don't have to be fresh to be popular!

Real folk music as near as Columbus! KHS field-trippers clapped along to Peter, Paul & Mary's songs about freight trains, lemon trees and stewballs . . .

Dr. Cornholt's special assembly against irresponsible vandalisms in washrooms drew an enthusiastic response.

Thanks to parents for lending cars to transport Prom balloons.

When "Psycho" trisected Mr. Lutz's equipment, they didn't know whether to give him an "E" in Bio or an "A" in Geometry.

"How's your sister?" kwipped kanga-kut-ups. "Can I put my fern in her kreel?"

Kefauver Student Kouncileers' new "Suggestion Box" gave kanga-recommenders an excellent opportunity to work on good penmanship as well as good citizenship.

Who says club meetings have to be dullsville? KHS's Girls' Young Women's Junior Future Mothers and Wives doesn't!

We saw Germany, we saw France, we saw the Prendergast Lampreys get a good kick in the pants!

"Away" basketball games let orange-and-turquoisers meet high schoolers of many different colors including white and yellow and black and blue.

"Ah-dee-ose moo-cha-chose, vi-ya con car-nay. . . ." Kefauver's modern-as-tomorrow language lab helped today's students master the tongues of yesterday.

Kar Klub members learn all the ins 'n' outs of home auto repair.

Purdy Lee Spackle set a new school record when he dissected eight frogs, eight white mice, two hamsters, four gerbils, and the super's cat, and he wasn't even taking Bio!

Just when we thought we had 'em all down, Social Science's Mr. Dittwiley'd pop up with another one!

Maybe one-way halls would solve this serious traffic untidyness!

Free play periods at midday provided an opportunity to make new friends and learn sharing with others.

Thanks to the Athletic Department for JV Girls' Water Ballet.

Gifted with a head for homework, our AFS visitor carried a full load of subjects!

On their toes ball-play brought Kangaroo pigskinner fans to their feet when Prendergast High was rocked back on its heels by a spectacular signal interception by Flinch "Big Ears" Baxter.

Unfortunately, in a school, like in a real democracy, vandals often try to stuff their own two cents worth into the repository of good citizenshiphood.

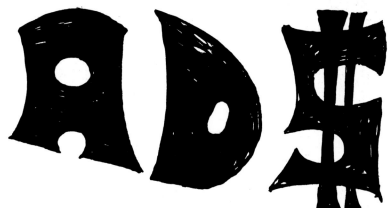

# PAW PRINTS

This Page Reserved For
Tammy Croup

# THE END
# OF OUR
# TAIL

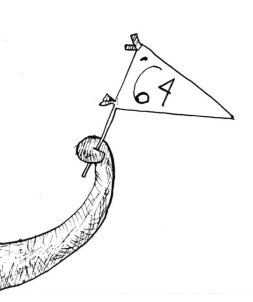

Hey LarryWannia "cream-filled"
Twinky?
(Twat you say? I cunt hear you the
first time. Bare-assed you again
or I'll have to finger it
out for myself!!!!)
See ya,
Wing-Ding!

Larry,

To a real sweet guy and I really mean that 'cause you're a swell guy and I mean that too !!! This has been a great year that we'll never forget and I hope we'll be able to remember it in the future together because of the great time we had. Boy we had a great time this year !!! Being only five desks apart from each other in Senior Study Hall was really great !!! Remember that time when we both came to the game open house ??? it and I won't ever forget either when you asked me to go to the Prom and boy did I have to rush to get my dress ready by 9 o'clock !! We really had some great times to- either at the Prom and at the Leaning Tower of Pizza after the Prom too !!! It pure was a shame you had to take me home early be- cause of all that homework you had to get done for Sunday but we really had lots of fun and I'll we have lots of fun this summer and 'cause I've got Mr. Beep-Beep-Beep to drive all summer and see you !!! come over and

all the time
X X X X X
O O O O
Eggy

HA-HA!
THE "MAD CLIPPER"
STRIKES AGAIN!

**KEFAUVER** ⊙ **HIGH SCHOOL**

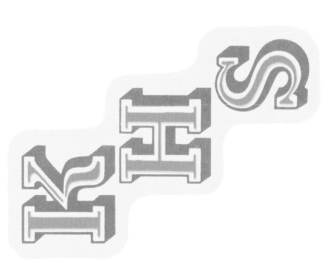

# 1963-1964
# BASKETBALL
# PROGRAM

**Buckeye COLA®**

Illegal flaming debris tossed from stands

Penalty, fighting

Time out to air gym

# HOME

| TEAM ROSTER | | Field Goals | Free Throws | Rebounds | Jumpshots | Pass-off to scores |
|---|---|---|---|---|---|---|
| Bob Baxter (F) | X | II | I | | | |
| Vince Lambretta (F) | | | | | | |
| Chuck Farley (G) | | | | | | |
| Bruno Grozniak (G) | | I | | | | |
| Madison A. Jones (C) | X | I | \ | | | |
| Gary Gerwin | | | | | | |
| Tom Sieler | | | | | | |
| Larry Sturton | | | | | | |
| Chuck Maypole | | | | | | |
| Hondo Vogel | | | | | | |

| SCORE: | 1st Quarter | 2nd Quarter | 3rd Quarter | 4th Quarter |
|---|---|---|---|---|
| | 10 | | | |

Public display of affection in stands

Visiting team wallets stolen from lockers

Illegal use of airhorn during free throws

Student auto in faculty parking place

Penalty, fighting in parking lot

Illegal use of ten-foot gym ceiling

**Buckeye COLA®**

Referee's child attends home school

Student spectator smoking in hall

Player with failing grades on court

## VISITORS — *St. Vitus*

| TEAM ROSTER | Personal Fouls | Traveling | Double Dribbling | 3-Second Violation | Goal Tending |
|---|---|---|---|---|---|
| Pete Czymszky | I | | | | I |
| Vito Manicotti | ꟼTI 1 | | | / | |
| John Belushi | I | | | | II |
| Dayle Murray | | | / | | I |
| Pat McNulty | HII II | | | | |
| Mike O'Rourke | | II | | I | IIII |
| Xaviera Ziti | | | | | I |
| Brian Mulligan | I | | | | I |
| Terry Klucher | | | | | I I |
| Tony Gentile | | | | | |

| SCORE: | 1st Quarter | 2nd Quarter | 3rd Quarter | 4th Quarter |
|---|---|---|---|---|
| | 39 | | | |

Time out to pump up ball

Towels on locker room floor

Open cola in gym

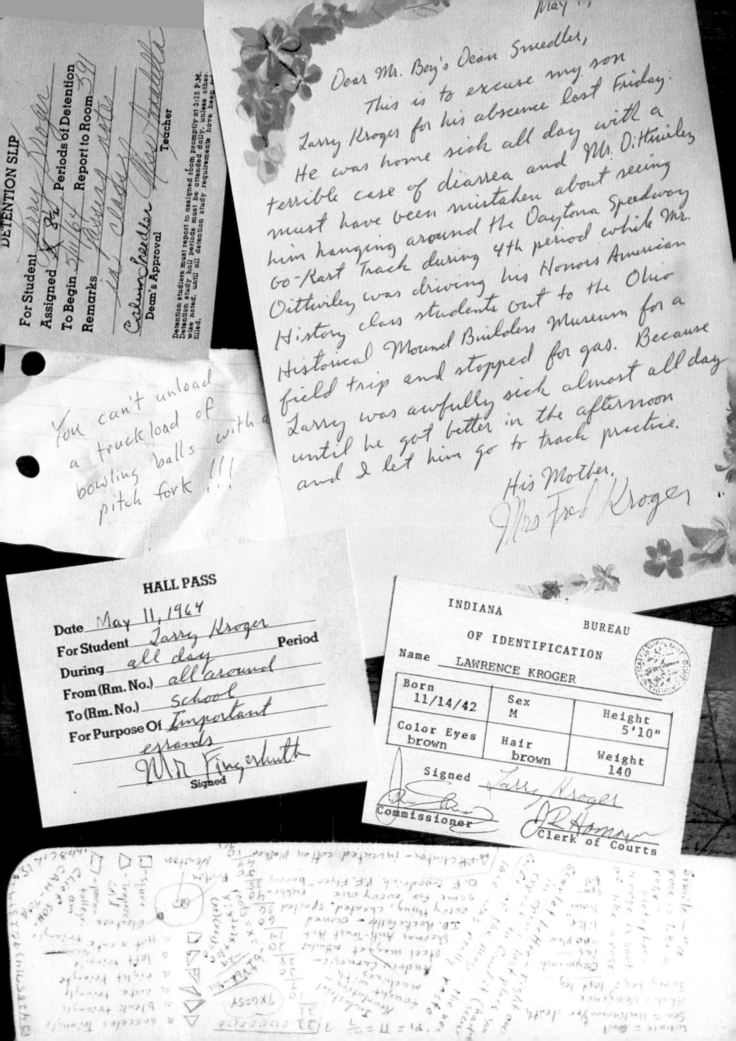

**DETENTION SLIP**

For Student _Larry Kroger_
Assigned by _8H_  Periods of Detention _1_
To Begin _5/11/64_  Report to Room _39_
Remarks _passing note_

_Calvin Snedler_  _Mrs Trabulk_
Dean's Approval  Teacher

Detention students must report to assigned room promptly at 3:15 P.M. Detention study hall periods must be attended daily, unless otherwise noted, until all detention study requirements have been filled.

---

May 11

Dear Mr. Boy's Dean Snedler,

This is to excuse my son Larry Kroger for his absence last Friday. He was home sick all day with a terrible case of diarrea and must have been mistaken about seeing him hanging around the Daytona Speedway Go-Kart Track during 4th period while Mr. Oithwiley was driving his Honors American History class students out to the Ohio Historical Mound Builders Museum for a field trip and stopped for gas. Because Larry was awfully sick almost all day until he got better in the afternoon and I let him go to track practice.

His Mother,
Mrs Fred Kroger

---

You can't unload a truckload of bowling balls with a pitch fork !!!

---

**HALL PASS**

Date _May 11, 1964_
For Student _Larry Kroger_
During _all day_  Period
From (Rm. No.) _all around_
To (Rm. No.) _School_
For Purpose Of _Important errands_

_Mr Fingerhuth_
Signed

---

**INDIANA**  **BUREAU**
**OF IDENTIFICATION**

Name  LAWRENCE KROGER

| Born 11/14/42 | Sex M | Height 5'10" |
| Color Eyes brown | Hair brown | Weight 140 |

Signed _Larry Kroger_
Commissioner  Clerk of Courts

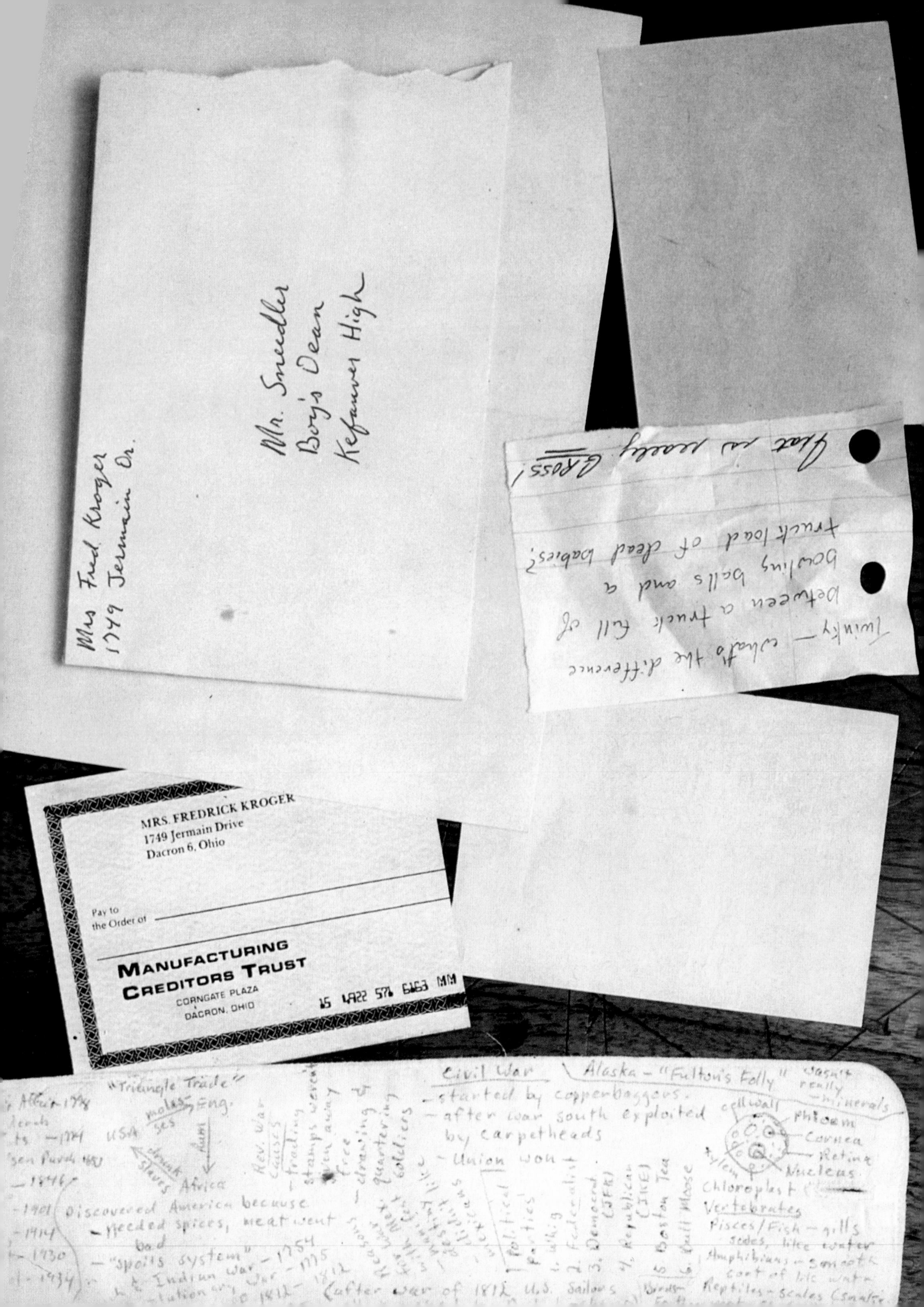

Mrs Fred Kroger
1749 Jermain Dr.

Mr. Sneedler
Boy's Dean
Kefauver High

Twinky — what's the difference
between a truck full of
bowling balls and a
truck load of dead babies?

Jack is really Gross!

---

**MRS. FREDRICK KROGER**
1749 Jermain Drive
Dacron 6, Ohio

Pay to
the Order of _____

**MANUFACTURING**
**CREDITORS TRUST**
CORNGATE PLAZA
DACRON, OHIO

15 4A22 576 6163 MM

---

"Triangle Trade"
molasses ← Eng.
Africa
slaves
rum

Civil War
- started by copperbaggers.
- after war south exploited
  by carpetheads
- Union won.

Alaska — "Fulton's Folly" Wasn't
really
minerals

cell wall
phloem
Cornea
xylem
Retina
Nucleus.
Chloroplast
Vertebrates
Pisces/Fish — gills
scales, like water
Amphibians — smooth
cool of his water
Reptiles — scales (snake)

Rev. War
causes
- trading stamps weren't
  given away free
- downsizing &
  quartering
  soldiers

Political
Parties
1. Whig
2. Federalist
3. Democrat (JFK)
4. Republican (IKE)
5. Boston Tea
6. Bull Moose

Albert 1748
- 1754 USA
- 1846
- 1901 Discovered America because
- 1914    - Needed spices, meat went
- 1930      bad
- 1934   - "spoils system" - 1754
            Indian war - 1775
         Revolution war - 1775
                    1812 (after war of 1812 U.S. sailors

# KEFAUVER

# HIGH SCHOOL

Twinky BR 2-6165

from - May 2
Call after Xmas

Larry Kroger

Lawrence Kroger

Lawrence Kroger

Lawrence Kroger

Lawrence Kroger

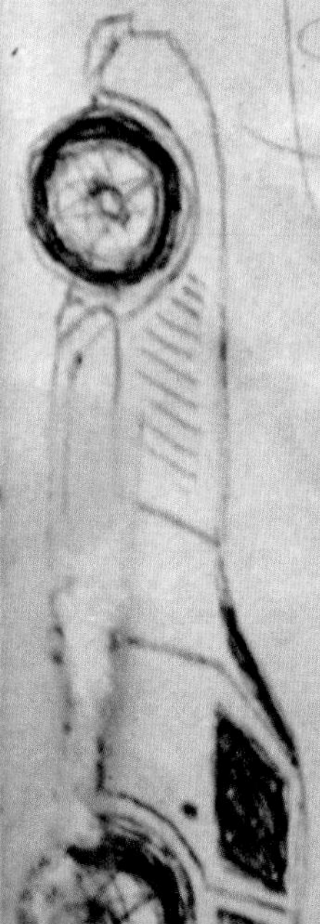

Larry "Lance" Kroger

Lance Kroger

Lance Kroger

Lance Kroger

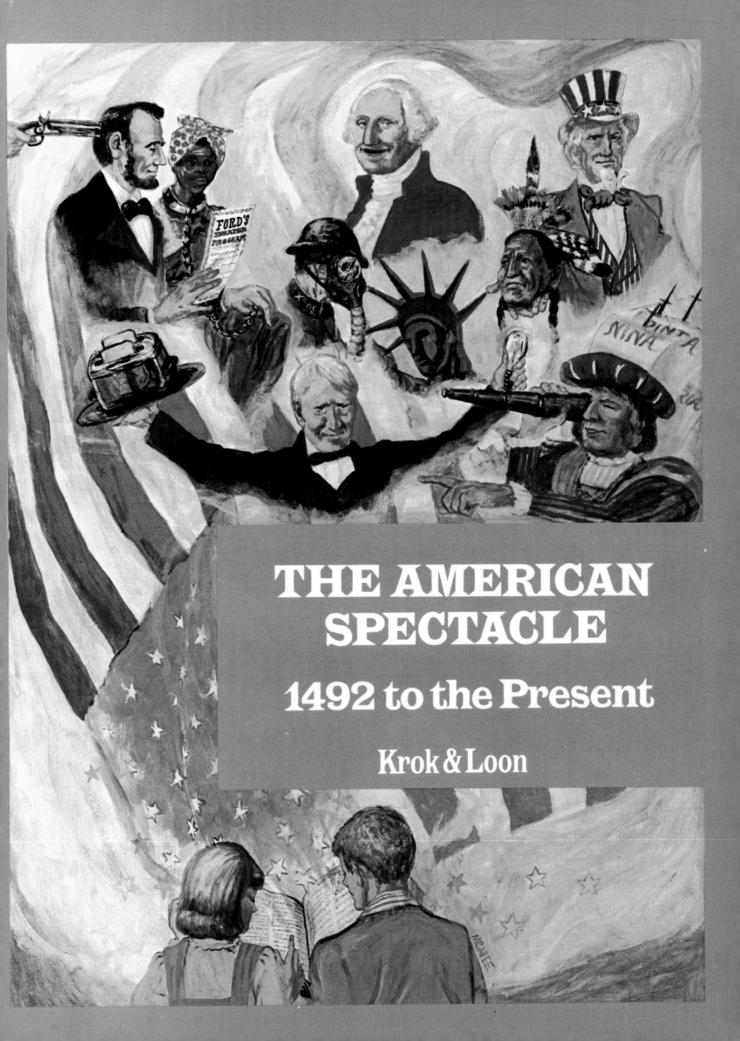

# THE AMERICAN SPECTACLE

## 1492 to the Present

### Krok & Loon

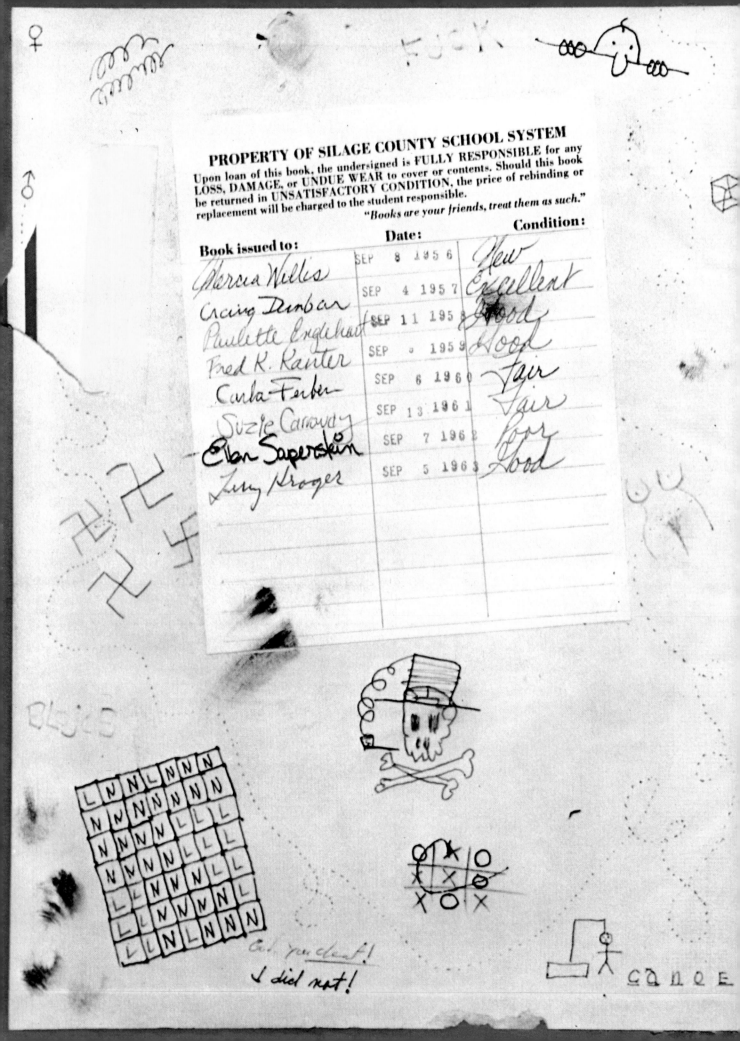

# PROPERTY OF SILAGE COUNTY SCHOOL SYSTEM

Upon loan of this book, the undersigned is FULLY RESPONSIBLE for any LOSS, DAMAGE, or UNDUE WEAR to cover or contents. Should this book be returned in UNSATISFACTORY CONDITION, the price of rebinding or replacement will be charged to the student responsible.

*"Books are your friends, treat them as such."*

| Book issued to: | Date: | Condition: |
|---|---|---|
| Marcia Willis | SEP 8 1956 | New |
| Craig Dunbar | SEP 4 1957 | Excellent |
| Paulette Englehart | SEP 11 1958 | Good |
| Fred K. Kanter | SEP 9 1959 | Good |
| Carla Ferber | SEP 6 1960 | Fair |
| Suzie Carraway | SEP 13 1961 | Fair |
| Ellen Saperstein | SEP 7 1962 | Poor |
| Terry Kroger | SEP 5 1963 | Good |

# THE AMERICAN SPECTACLE

## 1492 to the Present

**Henry W. Krok**
*Chairman, Dept. of Social Studies, Beloit College, Beloit, Wisconsin*

**Samuel D. Loon**
*Instructor of History, Lake Erie College, Painesville, Ohio*

© The MacMallard Publishing Company

Second Edition, 1949

Printed in Canada

# PREFACE

In the writing of this text, the authors have intended not merely to produce another dry compilation of musty facts, but to bring history to life for the student as a vital, continuing drama as fresh and fascinating as yesterday's newspaper. Through this volume, we have given the student the opportunity to acquaint himself with the main currents in the American historical process, a process which on the surface may often seem chaotic, even incoherent, until these events are maturely analyzed and placed in their proper headings, subheadings, and footnotes.

In addition, the authors have designed this volume to provide insight into the great movements associated with social intercourse, and that it may serve as a valuable tool in coming to grips with not only the past, but their future efforts as well.

Lastly, we hope that by reading *The American Spectacle*, the student will gain a greater appreciation of the forces and factors which led to America's taking its leading role in the postwar world, and by paying particular attention to important facts, dates, and footnotes, will not, like many unfortunates ignorant of high school level history, "be destined to repeat it" the following term.

## Preface to the Second Edition

The hurried march of events, including the remarkable reelection of President Truman and the dropping of the Iron Curtain's false face of friendship, plus the many kind letters we have received from students and educators alike concerning certain minor factual discrepancies in the original work, have made our dream of a second edition a reality. The most conspicuous changes in the text have occurred in the passages relating to William Jennings Bryan, the description of whose election as President in 1892 can only be attributed to printer's errors which found their way into the galleys during the many long, exhausting hours and weekends spent in the original collection and assemblage of materials.

In addition, the authors are more than ever keenly aware of their debt to other related texts and reference works through communications from teachers, writers, and legal representatives of similar publishing ventures all over the world, and hope that the deletion of chapters 4, 7, 8–11, and 13 and their replacement with innovative transparent overlays depicting elevation, population growth, rainfall, continental water tables, and the Rise of the Railroads will provide added visual interest for student and instructor alike.

Beyond this, changes in the text include addition of copyright notations inadvertently omitted due to printer's error from certain maps, charts, drawings, and photographs kindly provided by the related texts mentioned above. The page numbers, chapter headings, and all punctuation have been completely reset as well, adding, we trust, to greater clarity and ease of understanding as well as to this volume's purchase price.

Henry W. Krok
Samuel D. Loon

# CONTENTS

Twinky Kroger

Tammy Kroger

Tammy Croup Kroger

Mrs Tammy Kroger

Mr and Mrs Tammy Kroger

Mr and Mrs Larry Kroger

Mr and Mrs Larry

# CHAPTER ONE

# Hatching the Seeds of Democracy

*"Inne 1492, hie Sayled ye Oceanne Blewe . . ."*
—Sir Phillip Sidney

## Christopher Columbus, Marinator

The discovery of the New World by a bold Genoese navigator sailing under a snapping Spanish standard was not an isolated event, but one which took place against a rich and varied tapestry of factors, some crucially important, some so inconsequential as to walk a fine line between obscurity and irrelevancy. An entire galaxy of relations, some philosophic and economic, others religious, geographic, or technological, surround Columbus' achievement, each factor or cause clustering about this one momentous event like flies around a delicious Columbus Day sweetmeat.

First, there was the Renaissance to consider. With the reawakening of man's interest in the world around him, he began to challenge established beliefs in a flat world or imps dwelling in butter churns. New technological advances such as the compass aided exploration, as well as the map, the astrolabe, and the hull, this last innovation in shipcraft finally putting an end to seawater's natural tendency to seep into everything and dampen the spirit of exploration as surely as it did a crew's buns and sleepwear.

Secondly, Columbus believed that by sailing directly west from Spain, he would find a faster route to the spice-rich Orient and its treasure-trove of gold, cloves, precious stones, pepper, silk, and bay leaves, valued by Europeans both for its medicinal value as well as its curative powers. It is recorded, too, that even after his fourth unsuccessful return from the New World, the implacable adventurer still hoped to find the legend-enshrouded "Garlic Mines of King Solomon," which he believed lay somewhere between Wilmington and Dover. Authorities today doubt that the mines ever existed, but if they had, they would more logically have been located in the Azores, a fact which not a few prominent historians view as a blessing in disguise.

After his final voyage, Columbus returned to his Queen and patroness Isabella and presented her, a contemporary records, "wythe one grete Parrotte-Byrd boasting fyne Feathyrs & a foule Tongue, three Salvages, verie lousie & phlyguematick, & sundrie ynscrib'd Flagon Coasters, but noe Gold eythire in Barres, Amulets, nor sympel Nougates." Colum-

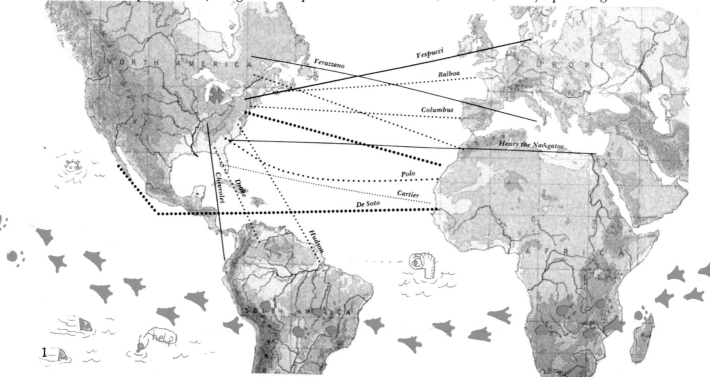

1

bus died penurious and alone, a broken man, which many in the Aragon court considered only appropriate.

It would be resorting to hindsight to say that Columbus was ill-advised to insist that North America was India after repeated voyages should have proven otherwise, much less to infer from this he was an incompetent moron, but credit must be given to this courageous seafarer among whose greatest accomplishments can be added not discovering King Solomon's Garlic Mines.

## Go West, Wretched Refuse

If Columbus' dream returned empty-handed, later ships anchored off the strange new shore freighted with destiny and later, human cargoes, although the lure of free land eventually attracted many Dutch, Welsh, Swedes, French Huguenots (*hugue*-nose), plus a smattering of Slavs, Serbs, Croats, Magyars, Svals, Smegyars, and Groats to sweeten the melting pot.

The ships transported a number of Finns and Poles in steerage as well, but these were normally lured aboard with seductive tales of a wondrous land where warm woolen socks grew wild on bushes, and subsequently kept in the bilge as ballast. Often they made several round trips across the Atlantic before being deposited at their destination which, when their eyes adjusted to the light, more often than not proved to be the Mindanao Deep.

A veritable influx of new settlers came from Europe, many of them fleeing religious or economic persecution, the latter often taking the form of pursuit by cruel "bailiffs" who under the barbaric English codes pursued their victims demanding "payment" for "debts."

In 1620, a tiny ship sailed from Holland with 102 souls bound for the verdant Virginia colony. Landing in rocky Plymouth, Massachusetts, the Mayflower's passengers disembarked, surveyed their new home, and stoned their navigator.

That first winter was hard, but when spring finally arrived a friendly Indian named Squanto who had seen the arrival of their "great canoe with laundry drying in tree-tops" showed them how to plant corn, first by inserting a kernel and putting in three fish as fertilizer. This method was later improved by the pilgrims themselves by deleting the fish and replacing them with three Indians.

Imagine the festive scene that first Thanksgiving must have presented! The harvest had been a fine one, and the oaken tables fairly groaned under the weight of the new world's bounty which included steaming bowls of yams, great trenchers of fresh rutabagas, whole cauliflowers, hot buttered flaxbread, broccolis, sweet-and-sour potatoes, roasted burdocks, wild thistles, acorn squash, chard, eggplant, kohlrabi, cowpeas, okra, wild turnips, curdled deer cheese, and many other "modern" favorites.

It is surprising that the myth of the "Thanksgiving Day turkey dinner" still enjoys such widespread popular acceptance. In point of fact, turkeys did not appear in North America until over 150 years later when, in 1774, Benjamin Franklin bred the first eating tom by crossing a chicken with a pig.

## Ninety-nine and Forty-four One-hundredths Percent Puritan

As the Massachusetts Bay colonies developed, the rugged character of Puritanism dominated the atmosphere of the region, particularly since wasting water by bathing was considered a worse sin than sleep. The Puritans were followers of Calvinism, named for John Calvin, a Swiss cheese burgher who preached "precrastination," which denied the efficacy of good works in attaining salvation, thus breaking dramatically with the Roman Church, which made occasional exceptions for money orders.

*Religious persecution in Europe drove many peoples to the new world in search of religious freedom. During the St. Anselm's Day Unpleasantness of 1623 depicted above, 302,000 Jehovah's Witnesses were slaughtered in fifteen minutes by Amish made berserk by mind-altering bread molds.*

Dour of demeanor, Calvinists frowned on singing, dancing, smoking, giggling, note-passing, and "alle manyeres of vaiyne & ydylle *Phancie*, esquyrminge in ye *Pewes*, alle *Phydgetynge*, unnecessarie blynckynge of Eiyes & vyle or naughtie *Pracktys* beeneathe ye *Coverlyttes*," not to mention spelling. They also frowned on frowning which left them little leeway for amusements or hobbies, having to "make do" with facial ticks, skin eruptions, and disease.

The Puritans left a rich cultural legacy to the American character, perhaps their most important bequests to us being the "Yankee trader" tradition, wooden nutmegs, witch hunts, eggnog, and mental illness. Their distinctive "pilgrim" hats can still be seen on route signs along many of Massachusetts' state and local thoroughfares.

Although their contribution was not as lasting as that of the English or the Dutch, the Swedish colonies off the coast of what is now Delaware once proved a potent force in America's early develop-

*"Care for a fish fritter, chief?" Dinner diplomacy was a common method for early English settlers to win the confidence of their red brothers. Traditionally, the Indians were made drowsy with teaberry brandy and then fed fish fritters with "surprise centers" consisting of a flat steel strip coiled under tension and released by stomach acids into a fifteen-inch cutting edge. Messy but effective.*

ment. "New Sweden," located on the St. Vikovic Islands, quickly rose to trading dominance among the Atlantic colonies. Backed by the might and prestige of the far-flung Scandanavian empire, New Sweden soon had a virtual stranglehold on the world's output of carved birds, fruit soups, enameled handicrafts, and little-meatballs-on-toothpicks, this last innovation in the traditional little meatball being made possible by the new world's millions of acres of virgin lumber.

New Sweden, in part financed by Ivor Kruger, the "Swedish match king," rapidly erected major trading centers on the Vikovics. The largest of these, Sverdluuntøwn, was situated on the island of St. Bfüderølf, and had it not sunk in a storm somewhere off the coast of North Carolina (with a supposed 10,000,000 krøner in little-meatballs-on-toothpicks yet unsalvaged), history might have followed a different path, and the very text you are mutilating with ballpoints and eargook at this very moment might well be peppered with slashed o's and your last name sound like a punctured concertina.

## "The Only Good Indian Is a Wood Indian"

By the early 1700s, the American Indian was increasingly hostile to the encroaching settlers, who in turn regarded the red men as rogue housepets or, at best, self-propelled garbage. Raids were common, and the outer fringes of a farm or plantation were frequently attacked, taking a heavy toll in honest yeomen and undentured servants, the taking of scalps having not yet been introduced by the French.

Settlers and Indians fought often and savagely, the Europeans using flintlocks and muskets while the Indians preferred their traditional "tomahawk" and "massacre." Possibly the most grisly of these early clashes was King Phillip's raid on a white settlement near what is today the Nu–Mart Shopping Plaza in Gritfield, Connecticut. There, on a quiet Sunday morning in early December, 304 Quakers were surprised by 11,000 Iroquois warriors and tortured, burnt, flayed, killed, raped, scalped, scraped, scalloped, harassed, and eaten by the raiding party which resented being left out of that first Thanksgiving dinner, although Iroquois were notoriously picky eaters and from the perspective of history had only themselves to blame.

To the south, colonies profited from another gift of the red man, tobacco, whose use and cultivation he taught in exchange for alcohol, religion and syphilis.

Slaves supplied the power to tend the large plantations and were considered a form of labor-saving device much in the same way you might consider your television set a person or God. Crammed into the same dank, airless holds once reserved for Finns and Poles, many Africans died in transit, often by suicide after having heard a southern accent for the first time. Survivors who reached Charlestown harbor were treated like so much meat, prodded, inspected, and often injected with artificial coloring and preservatives, scrawny Bantus frequently marked as choice Watusi or top grade mulatto.

Once sold, the slave's life was one of unending toil in the fields, harshly herded about by drivers, although to say that they were "treated like animals"

*A knock on the door in colonial times was not always a welcome occasion. Here a band of wild Indians are about to thank the settlers for a basket of Thanksgiving fish fritters sent for Thanksgiving. Though often poorly drawn, Indians were quite capable of mercy, and experts conjecture that they may have kept the one on the left around for awhile.*

is to do a disservice to the South's traditional respect for fine racehorses, who not only ate better than most slaves but were generally better educated.

## Untying the Mother Country's Umbilical Cord

Despite a general "hands off" policy, England's clumsy manipulation of the colonials' businesses increased friction, arousing and inflaming members,

*One of the first fruits of the British Stamp Acts, the above specimen was affixed to a postcard sent to Lafayette from General Cornwallis concerning a laundry or laundress (the handwriting is unclear) shared by the English commander and the famous French twit.*

who threatened to rise up and shoot their seamen.

Up until the 1760s, America was a willing part of the "mercantile system," an arrangement whereby the colonies sent raw materials to Britain in return for receipts, visiting dignitaries, and taxes. Increasingly restive about this, colonials marched through the streets of Boston shouting spontaneous slogans such as "No taxation without representation" and "Fie on unrestrained pow'rs presumed by Parliament in its cruel usages of her loyal but o'er-burthened subjects far frae' th' leaping waves!"

Sam Adams instigated these mobs, dubbed "Sons of Liberty" by the euphemistic British press, and staged mass protests, often playing a major role himself by prompting from behind a stout barrel or sturdy yeoman. The most famous of these demonstrations was the "Boston Tea Party," in which a band of men dressed as Indians boarded three British ships and dumped 300 sacks of tea and a deceptively sacklike cabin boy into Boston Harbor. It is said that this accounts for the slightly resinous flavor and brownish tinge of tapwater still served at the faithfully-preserved pubs and inns lining quaint, historic Washington Street.

In response to this, the British Parliament immediately voted the Intolerable Acts of 1773, followed quickly by the Repressive Acts of 1774, and finally, Parliament being what it is, the Unnatural Acts of 1776, these last measures also taking a stern view of colonials' cheek.

As hostilities increased, America was fortunate to be led by a group of remarkable men. Aristocratic Thomas Jefferson, a framer of the constitution and handy with upholstery, not to mention a wizard with leftovers, was the inventor of many useful devices. He devised the first folding pocket comb, the storm window, and an electric horse which might have changed the course of modern technology had

Benjamin Franklin, with whom Jefferson had quarreled, not refused to lend him sufficient current from a Leyden jar he kept under his wig. Monticello, designed by Jefferson, and believed to be the first building in North America with storm windows, was a classic of its time.

Franklin, a Philadelphia printer, served valuably as Ambassador to the Court of St. James and later, England and France. Here the portly aphorist delighted the French court with snippets from *Poor Richard's Almanac* like "Ring around the moon, go home soon" and impromptu "water harmonica" concerts on dinner goblets. It should be noted that the French court of the time may have enjoyed a considerably greater capacity for such delights than we do today.

Before his death in 1911, Franklin had invented the lightning rod, the Franklin stove, the bifocal lens, the Franklin waffle iron, and the storm door, which Jefferson took as a personal affront.

Lastly, George Carver Washington, called the "Father of His Country" by those unaware of what Jefferson did with his spare time, proved to be an able leader if difficult to understand through his wooden bridgework which legend has it he whittled himself out of cherrywood after his father punched his teeth out. His impeccable character made Washington an ideal President, and his imposing height plus an uncanny resemblance to a dollar bill struck a chord in his troops and made him an excellent rallying point on crowded and confused battlefields.

*While not a brilliant military tactician, George Washington excelled as a statesman and as a female impersonator, the latter talent putting the General in good stead with his men when, during their ordeal at Valley Forge, he entertained the troops with "bolde ditties & diversions." Washington died penurious and alone, plagued until the end of his days by psoriasis of the stomach and an almost constant semi-erection (see illustration).*

4

# The Shot Heard 'Round the Horn

On July 4th, 1775, a detachment of British regulars led by General Gage encountered a troop of "minutemen" at Lexington and Concord. Ordered not to fire until they saw the whites of their eyes, the American forces were unaware that a conjunctivitis epidemic had swept the redcoats' barracks the week before and the rebels were easily dispersed.

So it was that the dam erupted, and the American Revolution flexed its wings, borne on a wave of inflammatory grievances and ignited by the thirst for freedom.

In the next chapter we will see how the rebels sought popular support in the ensuing conflict, and how, from the heady early victories at Guernsey Creek and Flushing Meadows to the dark days at Valley Forge, the American people ran around like a bunch of chickens with their heads cut off until the British finally got fed up and the French agreed to pull our chestnuts out of the fire.

*"To arms! To arms! The British are coming!" These words shouted from horseback electrified the New England countryside as Paul Revere warned of the imminent English invasion. It is a little-known fact that "Paul Revere's ride" was undertaken largely on foot, Revere's mount Dave, the Wonderhorse, having died of a stroke while parked at a light.*

---

## Mastering What You Have Learned

### In Your Notebook
1. What were the sea dogs? Was it difficult to walk one?
2. Why were missionaries so eager to convert the Indians? How did their converters work? Steam powered?
3. When was the House of Burgesses founded? Was it ever losted?
4. When Patrick Henry said "Give me liberty or give me death," was he serious? Sober? Can you be sure?
5. Of all the massacres you have studied thus far in the term, which is your favorite? Write a report of a massacre as it might have appeared in *The New York Times.* Then, write one as it might have appeared in *The National Enquirer.* Do not show it to your teacher.

### Unrolling the Map
1. Reproduce for display a map of the world as it was known by the Ancient Greeks. Now make one as it is known by the Modern Greeks. How do you account for the similarity?
2. On an outline map of the United States, color in the parts of the country where they say "frappe" for milkshake and call soda "tonic" and serve it warm without ice.
3. On the same map, plot the major military campaigns of the French & Indian War. Now, taking a sheet of wax paper, place it over a modern road map of the same area and trace in colored pencils all the four-lane interstate highways running through the region. Then make a flour and water contour representation of the entire scene on the kitchen table. When you are finished, blame the mess on a little brother or sister.

### Food for Thought
1. What was George III's real last name?
2. If the Indians had the atomic bomb, do you think they would have used it? Would you?
3. Why did the colonists drill on the village greens? Do you feel this shows a disrespect for all vegetables? Some vegetables?
4. If Sam Adams was considered an agitator, how did he escape being made into handbags by the British? Discuss.
5. Who were the Quakers? Where did they get the idea for puffed oats? Was there any basic contradiction between their pacifist creed and having their puffed oats "shot from guns"?
6. Much of the Preamble to the Declaration of Independence can be found in the work of John Locke. Do you suppose Thomas Jefferson's desk was behind his in class? Would you have told on him?
7. The founding fathers stated "all men are created equal." Do you think they were serious? Or what?
8. John Adams once wrote, "The Revolution was effected before the war commenced. The Revolution was in the minds and hearts of the people." Was *he* serious? Was he running for anything at the time?

### Class Activities
1. Draw up a list of grievances and present it to your parents or teacher. Does this help you understand their usefulness? If you wish, you and your class may want to draw up a declaration of war.
2. Quote an appropriate maxim from *Poor Richard's Almanac* every time you observe someone in need of advice. How long do you suppose it will be before your teeth are punched out?
3. Divide your class equally into "patriots" and "tories." Designate one "tory" to be a "British tax collector" and tar and feather him. (Note: If tar and feathers are not available, you may substitute white paste and bits of torn construction paper.)

### Brain Teaser
1. What do you think the outcome of the Revolutionary War would have been if George Washington had been born a horse?

Miss Hampster
English IV
Rm. #233

(Name) Larry Kroger

Period 3

D+
Very poor work! I'm frankly a little surprised...

ENGLISH IV FINAL TEST

Directions: In each of the following sentences fill in the blank with the word or phrase that best completes the sentence. Keep your eyes on your own paper and do your own work.

X 1) In The Scarlet Letter, the man responsible for Hester Prynne's child Pearl was Nathanial Hawthorne

X 2) Pip's benefactor in Dickens' Great Expectations was named ~~Alagnet Sandwich~~. Micheal B. Anthony

X 3) A young boy and a poor slave meet two rascally scalawags called "the Duke and the Dauphin" in Mark Twain's famous novel "The Prince & the Pauper".

Very funny... X 4) "The woods are lovely, dark and deep" in the poem by Robert Frost, " Frosty the Snowman ."

X 5) Queequeg's two fellow harpooners in Herman Melville's Moby Dick were named ~~Quee~~ Tonto and ~~Pronto~~ Zorro .

X 6) In Edgar Allan Poe's poem "The Raven," the narrator is told that he will see his lost Lenore "at the dance."

X! 7) In William Shakespeare's play Romeo and Juliet, a feud is being fought between the Jets and the young at heart.

½ ✓ 8) Keats' famous poem, "Ode on a Grecian Urn," ends with the observation, "Beauty is truth, truth beauty,-- that is all ye know on earth, and that's all there is to it."

"all ye need to know."

While in other fine plays by Shakespeare his view of "politics" is often hard to put your finger on, in *Macbeth* which I enjoyed reading and rereading it is not.

**AWK!**

To prove this, one must support one's findings by citing the <u>specific scenes</u> and <u>quotations</u> the main character in "Macbeth" makes in regard to <u>his own</u> feelings about "ambition" not to mention "politics" ... scenes and quotations often too numerous to mention in an essay of this type but which will be listed below, time permitting.

**WHAT?!**

While there is no reason to believe that Shakespeare <u>himself</u> was ever involved in politics or ran for any office besides Bard of Avon, the ~~the~~ key to the complex relationship between *Macbeth*, "ambition," "politics." and "thanes" might well be found by turning our attention to a <u>specific scene</u> ... the "scene" of the play itself which the audience or careful rereader knows by the title alone is ~~Scot~~ ~~Ireland~~ Scotland.

Ambition, considered by many as either a good or a bad trait, is treated in *Macbeth* in much the same way that "the Bard of Avon" deals with many other character traits in this and his many other fine plays.

**Irrelevant**

Scotland, even in Shakespeare's time, was known for its excellent plaid kilts and "penny pinching" misers, that is, men who valued <u>money</u>, which can only be made in great quantities by <u>ambition</u>! (cont. on back of 2nd page of test)

9)  The character Willy Loman in Arthur Miller's play
    Death of a Salesman wishes to be "well *groomed* ."
10) In Edwin Arlington Robinson's poem "Richard Corey,"
    the title character, though rich and "imperially slim,"
    one day surprises the town by *gaining weight* .


ESSAY QUESTION


    It has been said that Shakespeare's Macbeth is not
so much a tale of a thane's ambition as it is a lesson in
politics.  Agree or disagree with this statement citing
specific scenes and quotations and support your findings
with direct references from other works you have read this
year.  Use the back of this test and your own paper, should
you need more room.

"Macbeth": Ambitious or Politician?

That the great William Shakespear's famous play "Macbeth" (which I may add is one of my personal favorites) is "not so much a tale of a thane's ambition as it is a lesson in politics" is a statement that may be easily agreed or disagreed with. Remarkably enough, the ~~real~~ answer to this question has a great deal to do with how ~~Shakesp.~~ the playwrite might have felt about "ambition" and "politics" himself!

Certainly, as the world's most famous writer, Shakespeare himself must have had some "ambition," but is it the same "ambition" felt by the thane mentioned above? I think not. Shakespeare's feelings about "politics" are not so clearly observed.

(cont. on back of 1st page of test)

Page 3

Thus, while in an essay of this type, with its highly limited amount of time and space, it is difficult to "agree" or "disagree" with the original quotation, it is safe to say that the play is neither so much a play about "Politics" or "ambition" as it is about ~~primarily, as a whole,~~ ourselves.!  ~~drama~~  ~~Shakespeare~~

SP

why?

As for the numerous scenes, quotations and references to the many other wonderful works we read and re-read this year, perhaps the most important of the long list to follow (time permitting) is when the main character in "Macbeth" in the final act where he is present, dramatically says to another character (though actually speaking to himself), "

references?
quotes?
other works?

TIME

| For Pupil | Last Name | First Name | Middle Name | File No. 2786156176 |
|---|---|---|---|---|
| | KROGER | LAWRENCE | CARROLL | Initiated: *Sept 6 1952* |

Grade School(s) Attended: *Burnside 1952-54* Dates, *McKinley 1954-60* Dates

High School(s) Attended: *Kefauver 1960-* Dates

Street Address(es): *2638 Rosewood* Zone *4* Dates *1946-54*
*1149 Valencia Dr* Zone *6* Dates *1954*
Zone ___ Dates ___
Zone ___ Dates ___

For additional transfers or transfer info. outside D.P.S. system, see attached sheet(s) Form(s) T60 and/or T83

Recent Photograph

| Born | Sex | Height | Weight | Color Hair | Color Eyes | Identifying Marks | Sibling File(s) |
|---|---|---|---|---|---|---|---|
| *7/11/46* | *M* | *5'5"* | *130* | *Brown* | *Brown* | *Birthmark on rt. hip* | *1-690571238* |

## RACIAL STATUS

- ☐ Negro, Mulatto, or Colored Acknowledged ☐ yes ☐ no
- ☐ American Indian
- ☐ Oriental
- ☐ Hindu or Arab (Includes Syrian & Lebanese)
- ☐ Jew
- ☐ Adopted
- ☐ Has ☐ Has not realized or made discovery
- ☒ White
- ☐ Other Specify ___

Is there evidence or possibility of dissimulation as to above status? ☐ yes ☒ no
Has pertinent information been forwarded to U.S. Bureau of Immigration and Naturalization?

## RELIGIOUS TRAINING

- ☐ Methodist
- ☐ Presbyterian
- ☒ Lutheran
- ☐ Episcopalian
- ☐ Other Specify and explain ___

Attendance ☐ Regular ☐ Sporadic ☐ Rare

## HOME ENVIRONMENT

Built *1954*
Cost $ *7,580.00*
Rms. *6*
Toilets *1½*
Lot Size *66 X 40*
No. Trees *1*
Garage *1 car*
Fin. Base. *yes*
Neighborhood ☐ "changing" ☒ stable

See Pupil Visitation Chart 4A

## CUMULATIVE TESTING DATA

| | | | |
|---|---|---|---|
| IQ Terman | *112** | | |
| IQ Wechsler | *106* | | |
| Rorschach | *AE* | *mild* | |
| Pol. Psych. Eval. | *NN* | | |
| Jr. Schol. Curr. Evt. | *68%* | | |
| Pres. Phys. Fit. | *Cert.* | | |
| Kuder Pref. | | | |
| PSAT | | | |
| Nat. Merit | | | |
| SAT Verbal | *356* | | |
| Math. | *420* | | |
| Eng. | | | |
| Science | | | |
| Hist. | | | |
| Lang. | | | |

**Remarks:**
* *(IQ Ter.) 3/11/53*
*stated parent had told him "wasn't just a game"*

## FAMILY BACKGROUND

Mother's Maiden Name: *Dorothea Margaret Checkly* First Middle Last Real Age *41*

### ROLE MODEL DEPORTMENT

- ☐ Working mother
- ☐ Previous marriages
- ☐ Excessive dress or makeup
- ☒ Cigarettes
- ☐ Miscarriages
- ☐ No church or charity work
- ☐ Fidelity problems
- ☐ Etiquette difficulties
- ☐ Female trouble
- ☐ Poor language or diction

Father's Name: *Fredrick Clifford Kroger* First Middle Last Changed From *Kroggershe*

OCCUPATION ☐ White Collar Specify *Foreman, Van Husen Corp.* ☐ Civil Service or Military Specify ___ ☐ LABORER

### FINANCIAL SECURITY

Wkly Salary $ *165.39*
Take-Home Pay $ *146.59*
Mort. Debt $ *8492.83*
Other Debts $ *1561.40*
Sav Acc. $ *1920.35*
Check. Acc. $ *115.00* (Avg.)
Stock, Bonds, & Other Invest. $ *250.00*
Mort. Equity $ *7100.00*
Other Prop. $ *300.00*
Net Worth $ *1024.00*

## WAR RECORD

- ☐ Volunteered for combat
- ☒ Failed to volunteer for combat.
- ☐ Other (attach record of court-martial proceedings)

H.U.A.C. File No. *281-42-1608*

## COMMUNITY CONDUCT

- ☐ Progressive Productivity
- ☒ Peak of Earning Power
- ☐ Tenuous Employ

Informants:
☒ Neighbors ☐ Associates ☐ Employer ☐ XEX

Police, employers, landlords, administrators, military, and other authorized personnel requesting copies of D.P.S.S. Permanent Records—please indicate past pupil's full name and year of graduation or transfer, if possible.

## INSTRUCTOR'S YEARLY PUPIL GROWTH

**Grade** 1    **Teacher** Mrs Frem    **Yr.** 52

General Academic Appraisal: B−    Overall Citizenship Evaluation: B+

Times Tardy: O    Fidgeting or Talking Out of Turn: Occasional

Comments: Picks nose and eats it

Have you visited pupil's home? ☐ yes ☒ no.
If "yes," complete appropriate sections of Chart 4A.

**Grade** 3    **Teacher** Miss Olson    **Yr.** 5_

General Academic Appraisal: C    Overall Citizenship Evaluation: C

Times Tardy: 5    Fidgeting or Talking Out of Turn: Very B_

Comments: Eats Paste

Have you visited pupil's home? ☐ yes ☐ no.
If "yes," complete appropriate sections of Chart 4A.

**Grade** 5    **Teacher** Mrs Arkwright    **Yr.** 5_

General Academic Appraisal: C−    Overall Citizenship Evaluation: B−

Times Tardy: 1    Fidgeting or Talking Out of Turn: a little too m_

Comments: Does not keep tidy desk - may not be college material

Have you visited pupil's home? ☒ yes ☐ no.
If "yes," complete appropriate sections of Chart 4A.

---

## DACRON MUNICIPAL POLICE
### Juvenile Division Record

**Form 90** Forward to Adult Offenders

**Section** 7/11/64

Scout Troop Bldg. Tour Prints

| Thumb | Forefinger | Middle Finger | Third Finger | Fourth Finger |

**Name** Kroger (Last)   Lawrence (First)   city (Middle)

**Address** 1749 Jermain

**Father's Phone at Work** FR 6-7700

**CASE**

### APPREHENSION

8/17/54—repeatedly called to come in house, would not leave stoop game

1/9/58—with snowballers, Church window broken Upton & North Cove

9/4/52—changed lanes without signalling, Monroe St &

### DISPOSITION

mother called Officer Friendly on phone

Officer Friendly Rev. Otis Peterson

Bed without dinner, no TV for a week

Payed share of damages out of sav.

X   $25 fine.

Officers Charles &

---

## MEDICAL REPORT SYNOPSIS

For complete details see attached sheet Form M544.

**VACCINATIONS**

- ☒ Smallpox Date 11/47
- ☒ Polio Date 4/57
  - ☒ Salk ☐ Sabin
  - ☐ Control Group Placebo
- ☒ Tetanus (within last 18 mos.)
- ☐ Leukemia
- ☐ Typhoid

**CHILDHOOD DISEASES**

| | | | | |
|---|---|---|---|---|
| 1 ☒ Chicken Pox | 5 ☒ German Measles | 9 ☐ Ringworm |
| 2 ☐ Diphtheria | 6 ☒ Mumps | 10 ☐ Scarlet Fever |
| 3 ☐ Impetigo | 7 ☒ Pinkeye | 11 ☒ Tonsilitis |
| 4 ☒ Measles | 8 ☒ Pinworms | 12 ☐ Whooping Cough |

Remarks: (8)—persistent rectal itch, tests neg.
(5) 10/57—Cousin Sheila Kroger, 6 lb. boy, no arms

**GENERAL**

- ☐ Moles or Warts
- ☒ Dandruff
- ☒ Acne Pimples Socially debilitating ☐ yes ☒ no
- ☐ Dental Cavities
- ☐ Halitosis
- ☒ Athlete's Foot
- ☐ Body Odor
- ☐ Mouth Breather
- ☐ Obesity
- ☐ Blackhead Pores
- ☐ Bed-wetting
- ☐ Bad Posture
- ☐ Poor Coordination

This is to certify that the above information and other information attached is true to the best of my professional knowledge and that all information here entered or attached has been transferred in the strictest confidence to this municipal file under the privileges and obligations of the Physician-School Board relationship as ordered by custom and law.

_____
Doctor's Signature

---

## PERSONAL HYGIENE

### BODY

| | Poor | Fair | Good | Excel. |
|---|---|---|---|---|
| 1. Breath | | | ☒ | |
| 2. Ears | | | ☒ | |
| 3. Eyes | | | | ☒ |
| 4. Face | | ☒ | | |
| 5. Feet | | ☒ | | |
| 6. Gums | | | ☒ | |
| 7. Hands | | | ☒ | |
| 8. Hair | | | ☒ | |
| 9. Nails | | ☒ | | |
| 10. Nose | | | ☒ | |
| 11. Perspiration | ☒ | | | |
| 12. Private Parts | | | | |
| 13. Spittle | | ☒ | | |
| 14. Teeth | | | ☒ | |
| 15. Eating Habits | ☒ | | | |
| 16. Friends | | ☒ | | |
| 17. Language | | ☒ | | |
| 18. Pastimes | | | ☒ | |
| 19. Toilet Habits | | | | |

### BELONGINGS

| | Poor | Fair | Good | Excel. |
|---|---|---|---|---|
| 20. Athletic Equip. | | | ☒ | |
| 21. Books | | | ☒ | |
| 22. Desk Tops | | | ☒ | |
| 23. Exams | | | ☒ | |
| 24. Gym Clothes | | ☒ | | |
| 25. Gym Locker | | | ☒ | |
| 26. Homework | | | ☒ | |
| 27. Jewelry | | | | |
| 28. Locker | | | ☒ | |
| 29. Lunch Bucket | | | ☒ | |
| 30. Notebooks | ☒ | | | |
| 31. Outerwear | | | ☒ | |
| 32. Pens and Pencils | | | ☒ | |
| 33. Shirts/Blouses | | | ☒ | |
| 34. Shoes | | ☒ | | |
| 35. Slacks/Skirts | | | ☒ | |
| 36. Socks/Hose | | ☒ | | |
| 37. Sweaters | | | ☒ | |
| 38. Underwear | | SEE #12 | | |

Remarks: #12 Improvement may be shown. No recurrence since '55.

Is school physical plant equipped with dual way mirrors?
☒ yes ☐ no

# INSTRUCTOR'S YEARLY PUPIL GROWTH SURVEY

Grade _7_ Teacher _Mr. Seadle_ Yr._58-9_

General Academic Appraisal _C-_    Overall Citizenship Evaluation _D_

Times Tardy _4_    Fidgeting or Talking Out of Turn _Constantly_

Comments _looked up a girl's skirt._ _Intentionally drops his pencils._

Have you visited pupil's home? ☐ yes ☒ no.
If "yes," complete appropriate sections of Chart 4A.

---

Grade _8th_ Teacher _Mrs. Lavender_ Yr._59-60_

General Academic Appraisal _C-_    Overall Citizenship Evaluation _D+_

Times Tardy _6_    Fidgeting or Talking Out of Turn _all the time!_

Comments _Picks at himself_

Have you visited pupil's home? ☐ yes ☒ no. !
If "yes," complete appropriate sections of Chart 4A.

---

Grade _9_ Homeroom Advisor _Mr. D. Postum_ Yr._60-1_

General Academic Appraisal _C_    Overall Citizenship Evaluation _C_

Times Tardy _2_    Fidgeting or Talking Out of Turn _fidgets_

Comments _Spontaneous penile arousal during 2nd and 3rd periods. Occ. fails to shower after Phys. Ed._

Have you visited pupil's home? ☐ yes ☒ no.
If "yes," complete appropriate sections of Chart 4A.

---

Grade _10_ Homeroom Advisor _Mrs. E. Hampster_ Yr._61-62_

General Academic Appraisal _B-_    Overall Citizenship Evaluation _C_

Times Tardy _1_    Fidgeting or Talking Out of Turn

Comments _Gym - has looked at other boys while dressing._

Have you visited pupil's home? ☐ yes ☒ no.
If "yes," complete appropriate sections of Chart 4A.

---

Grade _11_ Homeroom Advisor _Mr. D. Nansburter_ Yr._62-3_

General Academic Appraisal _C+_    Overall Citizenship Evaluation _C+_

Times Tardy _3_    Fidgeting or Talking Out of Turn _dying of hygiene_

Comments _Folder wore brown shoes with blue suit to PTA meeting_

Have you visited pupil's home? ☐ yes ☒ no.
If "yes," complete appropriate sections of Chart 4A.

---

Grade _12_ Homeroom Advisor _Miss Patella_ Yr._63-4_

General Academic Appraisal _D_    Overall Citizenship Evaluation _C-_

Times Tardy _14_    Fidgeting or Talking Out of Turn

Comments _His language among peers indicates sexual misinformation._

Have you visited pupil's home? ☐ yes ☒ no.
If "yes," complete appropriate sections of Chart 4A.

---

## PRIDE IN PERSONAL APPEARANCE
### Faults of Dress

| | Often | Occas. | Never |
|---|---|---|---|
| 1. Ankle bracelets | | | X |
| 2. Blue denim pants | | X | |
| 3. Boots or sandals | | | X |
| 4. Dark glasses | | X | |
| 5. Distracting jewelry | | | X |
| 6. Facial hair | | | X |
| 7. Heavy makeup | | | X |
| 8. Heel taps | | | X |
| 9. Immodest styles | | | |
| 10. Inappropriate objects | | X | |
| 11. Leather jackets | | | X |
| 12. Long or ratted hair | | | X |
| 13. Loud colors | | | X |
| 14. Net hose | | | |
| 15. No socks | | X | |
| 16. Odd expressions | | X | |
| 17. Tight pants | | X | |
| 18. Unusual shoes | | | X |
| 19. White lipstick | | | X |

Remarks _"sideburns" occasionally exceed ½"_

---

## SUMMER & AFTER SCHOOL EMPLOYMENT

| Date | Job | Fired | Quit |
|---|---|---|---|
| 6-8/59 | Mowed lawns | | |
| 6-8/60 | Mowed lawns | | |
| 6-8/61 | Mowed lawns | | |
| 6/62 | Dishwasher, Hamburg Heaven | | X |
| 6-8/62 | Mowed lawns | | |
| 5-8/63 | Van Husen Co., Stock Control | X | |

---

## SELECTIVE SERVICE CLASSIFICATION

Eligible _7/11/64_

Registered _____

☐ Draft
☐ Defer
☒ Decision pending 4th quarter grades

Local Draft Board No. 75
Morton Treacle, *President*,
Marie Corning, *Secretary*,
Shelton Polk,
Irwin Dewlap,
Samuel Quiggs,
Conrad Hopple,
L. Philip Gerwin.

Local Board No. 75
Silage County
New Federal Bldg.
234 Summit St.
Dacron 4, Ohio

| Interview Date | PSYCHOLOGICAL PROFILE | SERUM MEDICATION FOR PROBITY |
|---|---|---|

**SERUM MEDICATION FOR PROBITY**

☐ yes ✓ no

If yes, indicate interview date, chemical, and administrative mode.

Date_____

☐ Luminal
☐ Thiopental Sodium
☐ Digoxym
☐ Other (specify)

☐ Luncheon Period
☐ Parental Cooperation
☐ Doctor's Prescription
☐ Other (specify)

**Interview Date: 10/20/60**

Orientation Class – Routine Fresh Interview: norm to near norm Oedip. adj. Mild anal expulsive tend., see trauma on rec. – later therap. poss. Probable freq. auto-erotic contacts – guilt/avoidance in discussion. Libidinal activ: Causality provided for sporadic Superego Compensation – may keep rec. of a-ero act. to attempt willful reduc. Elaborate fantasy constructs (partly uninh. mature Modus vivendi) in persistence from earlier developmental stages ① pseudo-military, Super-ego-libido penile/aggressive ② id-libido anal/agressive, using automotive symbolology.

**3/9/63**

Persistent tardiness to class. Exhibits several neurasthenic symptoms and crypto-logophobic attitudes towards Hygiene Course. Prog: Suggested Therapy – assisted self-correction with cont. Detention Study Halls.

**11/25/63**

Fred. Gov. Survey ans: slight "loner" tend. further obser. indic.

**EVALUATION**

☐ Normal

☑ Near-normal
Armed Ser, Univ. Ad, employers note: to be observed

☐ Serious Disturbance (indicate):
☐ Shock Therapy
☐ Court Ordered Institutionalization

Dr. Martin Izing
Signature, School Psychiatrist

## CHART 4A—Pupil Home Visitation Report

| VISIT | DATE | GRADE | TEACHER | GROUNDS FOR VISIT |
|---|---|---|---|---|
| 1 | Feb. 25 | 3 | Mrs. Olson | Brought Homework (things) |
| 2 | Nov. 21, 1956 | 5 | Mrs. Arkwright | Social Call |
| 3 | Jan. 8, 1958 | 6 | Miss Herrington | Pupil had 3-day measles, delivered school work |
| 4 | | | | |
| 5 | | | | |
| 6 | | | | |

Please complete below information for each visit made.

Marking System:  No Mark —Satisfactory   U —Unsatisfactory   N —Not Observed
X —Seriously unsatisfactory situation or condition.  Proper authorities informed.

### ASPECTS OF THE HOME ENVIRONMENT

Additional Remarks (please indicate Visit No.)  #2 — bicycle left in driveway

Attach separate sheet Form 4A00 if total school system visits have exceeded six.
Note: Above information should not be applied to pupil's academic ratings in any manner other than that prescribed by D.P.S.S. regulations.

Hey Larry!
Look what fell out of
Twinky's notebook!
—Wing Ding

# ♡? SEX TEST ♡?

1. Have you ever been kissed on the lips? (YES) NO

2. Have you ever let a boy put his tongue in your mouth? YES (NO)

3. Have you ever let a boy put his tongue in your ear? YES (NO)

4. Have you ever let a boy put his tongue in your nose? YES (NO)

5. Have you ever kissed for more than 5 minutes? ~~YES~~ ~~No~~  *none of your business!*

6. Have you ever kissed a boy in your swimsuit? (YES) NO

7. Have you ever kissed a boy in your pajamas? YES (NO)

8. Have you ever kissed a boy in his underpants? YES (NO)  *ick!*

9. Have you ever let a boy put his hand on your sweater? (YES) NO

10. Have you ever let a boy put his hand on the front of your sweater? YES (NO)!!

11. Have you ever let a boy put his hand under your sweater over your bra under your blouse? YES (NO)

12. Have you ever let a boy take your bra off? YES (NO)

13. Have you ever had a bra? (YES) NO

14. Have you ever petted below the waist? ~~(YES)~~ ~~(NO)~~  *sort off... but not*

Wendy Ann Dempler
English
Mrs. Hamster, third period
May 1st, 1964 A.D.

Senior Essay:
"Old Man and the Sea": Fable or Tale?
In Ernest ~~Hemingway~~ ~~Hemmay~~ ~~Hemmww~~

15. Have you ever petted below the waist for more than 5 minutes?  YES (NO)

16. Have you ever let a boy put his hand under your shirt? YES N

17. Have you ever let a boy put his fingers you-know-where? (YES) NO

18. Have you ever let a boy put more than 5 fingers you? know-where?  YES (NO)

19. Have you ever gone all the way?  *wouldn't you like to know* YES ~~NO~~

20. Have you ever gone all the way for more than 5 minutes?  YES (NO)

## SCORE

| "Number of yeses" | What kind of girl you are |
|---|---|
| 0 | FRIGID |
| 1-2 | CAMPFIRE GIRL |
| 3-4 | TEASE |
| 5-6 | NICE GIRL |
| 7-8 | BAD GIRL |
| 9-10 | SEXY |
| 11-12 | REAL WOMAN |
| 13-14 | SOPHISTICATED |
| 15-16 | FAST & LOOSE |
| 17-18 | OVERSEXED |
| 19-20 | HOAR |

*Hey Larry! You know the difference between a "nice" girl and a "good" girl?*
*No. what?*
*A nice girl knows it's hard to be good and a good girl knows it's good to be hard to be good!*
*Cut it out Mr. Fortune's watching*

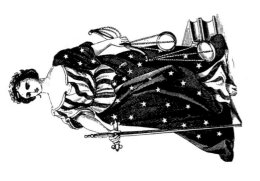

# DACRON PUBLIC SCHOOLS

## Pupil Growth Report—for grades 9 through 12

*Name* **Lawrence Kroger**

*Grade* __12__

*School* **C. Estes Kefauver High School**

*School Year* __1963-1964__

This report has been prepared to give parents a complete and accurate description of their child's ability, intelligence, integrity, future potential, and personal worth. Long experience has proven the veracity and reliability of the marking system used and such marks are an immutable matter of record.

Parents of pupils with an excellent report should be justly proud and to them the School System extends its congratulations. Pupils with average or normal marks have, on the other hand, been conclusively shown to lack exceptional ability in important physical and academic fields. This should not, however, be cause for dismay by pupils or parents. Steady employment and application may eventually reveal an aptitude or facility in some vocational field and thereby a productive and regular life may be led. Nor do average marks preclude a stable marriage and satisfying home life.

When a report shows very poor marks the fault lies with the pupil and he or she should be so informed. Not all like a doctor's report of malignancy, poor marks require immediate attention—in the form of increased discipline and removal of unproductive habits and companions. A conference with school officials will be found helpful to this end.

Alteration of or tampering with a Public School System Pupil Growth Report is a violation of the law punishable by a fine of not more than $2000 and imprisonment for not more than two years.

*Homeroom Advisor* __Miss Doris Critelli__

*Principal* **Dr. Humphrey Cornholt**

---

**Comments by Teachers or Principal:**

*Grading Period 1:* Lawrence's attendance and attention need the fun a bonus to do all.

*Grading Period 2:* Has not kept up with rest of class in personal hygiene habits and enthusiasm for current events.

*Grading Period 3:* I had hoped for more from Lawrence this semester.

*Grading Period 4:* We are expecting more tomorrow this year.

---

*Signature of Parents:*

*First Grading Period* Mrs. Fredrick Kroger

*Second Grading Period* Mrs. Fredrick Kroger

*Third Grading Period* Mrs. Fredrick Kroger

*Fourth Grading Period* Mrs. Fredrick Kroger

---

## Certificate of Pupil Growth

for year ending __June 7, 1964__

This is to certify that pupil __Lawrence Kroger__

has been promoted to grade _____ retained in grade _____

assigned to grade _____ graduated from grade __12__

in the Dacron Public Schools,

__Miss Doris Critelli__ —*Homeroom Advisor*

__C. Estes Kefauver High__ —*School*

*Philo T. Doherty*
*Superintendent of Schools*

## Pupil Study Habit Deficiencies Deportment Profile

| | Unsatisfactory | | | |
|---|---|---|---|---|
| | 1 | 2 | 3 | 4 |
| Cannot grasp main ideas | | | | |
| Gives insufficient attention to detail | | | ✓ | |
| Will not use own initiative | | | | |
| Does not work independently | | | | |
| Responds poorly to guidance | | | | |
| Fails to follow directions/helpful suggestions | | | | ✓ |
| Self-involved/prone to "primping" | | | ✓ | ✓ |
| Does not take pride in personal appearance | | | ✓ | ✓ |
| Does not participate in class discussions | | | | |
| Fails to raise hand before speaking | | | ✓ | |
| Refuses to join in group activities | | | ✓ | ✓ |
| Talks out of turn | | | | ✓ |
| Tries to be center of attention | | | | |
| Shy or withdrawn in social/class situations | | | | |
| Uncomfortable with fellow students | | | | |
| Talks to neighbor | | | | |
| Shows marked inability to involve him/herself in general, "give and take" | | | ✓ | ✓ |
| Disrupts classroom with personal views | | | | |
| Cannot communicate with peers in joint interactions | | | | |
| Given to "chattering" | | | ✓ | ✓ |
| Experiences difficulty in verbal interchange with classmates | | | | ✓ |
| Distracts other pupils with "comments" and "opinions" | | | | |
| Tends to be a "clockwatcher" | | | | |
| Experiences apparent difficulty telling time | | | | |

## Pupil Development Graph

— — —  Path of Normal Development toward Young Adulthood
. . . . . .  Path of Pupil's Development toward Young Adulthood

| | Grade School Development | High School Development |
|---|---|---|
| Grade | 1  2  3  4  5  6  7  8 | 9  10  11  12 |

- Achievement of General Young Adulthood
- Ambition and Appreciation for the Value of Property
- Recognition of Status and Position in Self and Others
- Mature Public Attitudes
- Social Reciprocation and Courtesy
- Reliable Deportment
- Obedience to Authority of All Types
- Emulation of Suitable Adults
- Efforts to Please Family and Organizational Superiors
- Respect for Adult Conventions
- Conformity to Peer Norms and Mores
- Maintenance of Cleanliness

---

| School Achievement | 1 Final Grade | 2 Final Grade | 3 Final Grade | 4 Final Grade |
|---|---|---|---|---|
| General Science | C+ | C | D | C |
| Practical Science | | | | |
| Biological Science | | | | |
| Chemical Science | | | | |
| Physical Science | | | | |
| Practical Physics | | | | |
| Practical Math | | | | |
| Basic Math Skills | | | | |
| Business Math | | | | |
| Algebra I, II | C- | D- | C- | |
| Plane Geometry | | | | |
| Solid Geometry | | | | |
| Plane and Solid Geometry | | | | |
| Trigonometry | | | | |
| English I, II, III, IV | B | C | D | C |
| Basic English Skills | | | | |
| Elementary English | | | | |
| Business English | | | | |
| Beginners English | | | | |
| Remedial English | | | | |
| Corrective English | | | | |
| Explanatory Writing | | | | |
| Speech | | | | |

| School Achievement | 1 Final Grade | 2 Final Grade | 3 Final Grade | 4 Final Grade |
|---|---|---|---|---|
| Spanish I, II, III, IV | C | | C | C |
| French I, II, III, IV | | | | |
| Latin I, II | | | | |
| American History | | | | |
| Ohio Government | | | | |
| Municipal Civics | | | | |
| Orientation | | | | |
| Living and Life | | | | |
| Family Posture I, II | | | | |
| Marriage Skills | | | | |
| Feminine Hygiene | | | | |
| Dramatic Theatre Arts | | | | |
| Music and Band | | | | |
| Music and Band Appreciation | | | | |
| Creative Artwork I, II | | | | |
| Physical Education I, II, III, IV | B | | B | C-B |
| Driver's Education | | | | |
| Vocational Arts | | | | |
| Manual Crafts | | | | |
| Auto Shop | | | | |
| Woodwork | | | | |
| Typing and Shorthand | | | | |
| Typing | | | F | D |

## Marking System

A — Pupil is doing very much better work than the ordinary students in his grade level.

B — Pupil is doing somewhat better work than the show students in this grade level but achievement is not superior.

C — Pupil is keeping pace with slow students in his grade level but is not exercising required effort or concentration.

D — Pupil is falling behind all students in his grade level due to lack of initiative and intelligence.

F — Pupil will be either held back at present grade level or expelled, according to his work in other grading periods.

## Attendance

| | 1 | 2 | 3 | 4 |
|---|---|---|---|---|
| Periods absent without excuse | 1 | 0 | 0 | 1 |
| Times tardy to school | 0 | 1 | 3 | 0 |
| Times tardy to class | 1 | 4 | 12 | 4 |
| Times tardy to extracurricular activities | 0 | 0 | 3 | 0 |

## Comments

# C. Estes Kefauver Memorial Higher School

### DACRON, OHIO

"CLEANLINESS"

"KNOWLEDGE"

"THRIFT"

"TEMPERANCE"

WHEREFORE BE YE CERTIFIED HEREWITH

**Lawrence Kroger**

HATH CONFERRED UPON HIM BY

## The Honorable Philo M. Duggerty, Superintendent of Schools

HAVING DUE RECOMMENDANT OF THE HIGHER SCHOOL PRINCIPAL THEREUPON AND TESTIFICATE, ADMINICLE, AND ATTESTATION THEREAS TO SATISFACTION IN ALL COMPLETEMENT OF PREREQUISITES EACH, BOTH OF PHYSIC AND ACADEMIC, FOR CAUSE OF GRADUATION AS PRESCRIBED BY HONOR AND LONG TRADITION AND THE DACRON BOARD OF EDUCATION AND HERETOFORE MERITS THIS

## DIPLOMA

IN WITNESS THEREFORE HEREBY WE FORTHWITH AFFIX THIS OUR SEAL

AND THESE OUR SIGNATURES UPON THE ____12th____ DAY OF ____June____

ONE THOUSAND NINE HUNDRED AND SIXTY ____4____

"BETTER CITIZENS THROUGH ORDERLY EDUCATION"

DACRON PUBLIC SCHOOLS

_President of the Board of Education_

_Superintendent of Schools_

HUMPHREY C. COBNOLT
_Principal of C. Estes Kefauver_

Treacle Printing Co., Dacron, Ohio

# SELECTIONS — POINT CONSENSUS

# HANDICAP PICKS — TROTTER SEL
## Results And Scratches

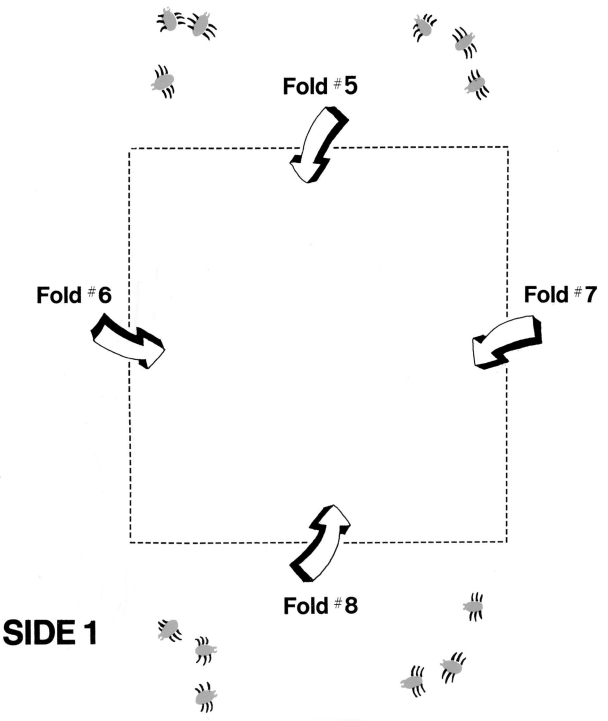

**Fold #5**

**Fold #6**

**Fold #7**

# SIDE 1

**Fold #8**

CUT ALONG HERE

# COOTIE CATCHER

### INSTRUCTIONS

**1.** Cut CATCHER out along "cut" lines. (Use razor blade for the hard one.)

**2.** Turn resulting square over to side #2.

**3.** Fold corners 1-4 to center as shown on back of these instructions.

**4.** Turn the smaller square over and fold 5-8 the same way so you have an even *smaller* square.

**5.** Insert thumb and first three fingers into the four pockets that are thus formed and fudge around until it looks like 5.

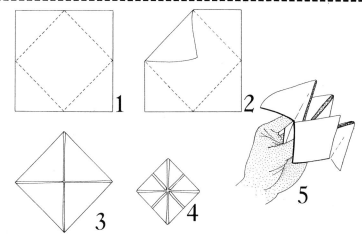

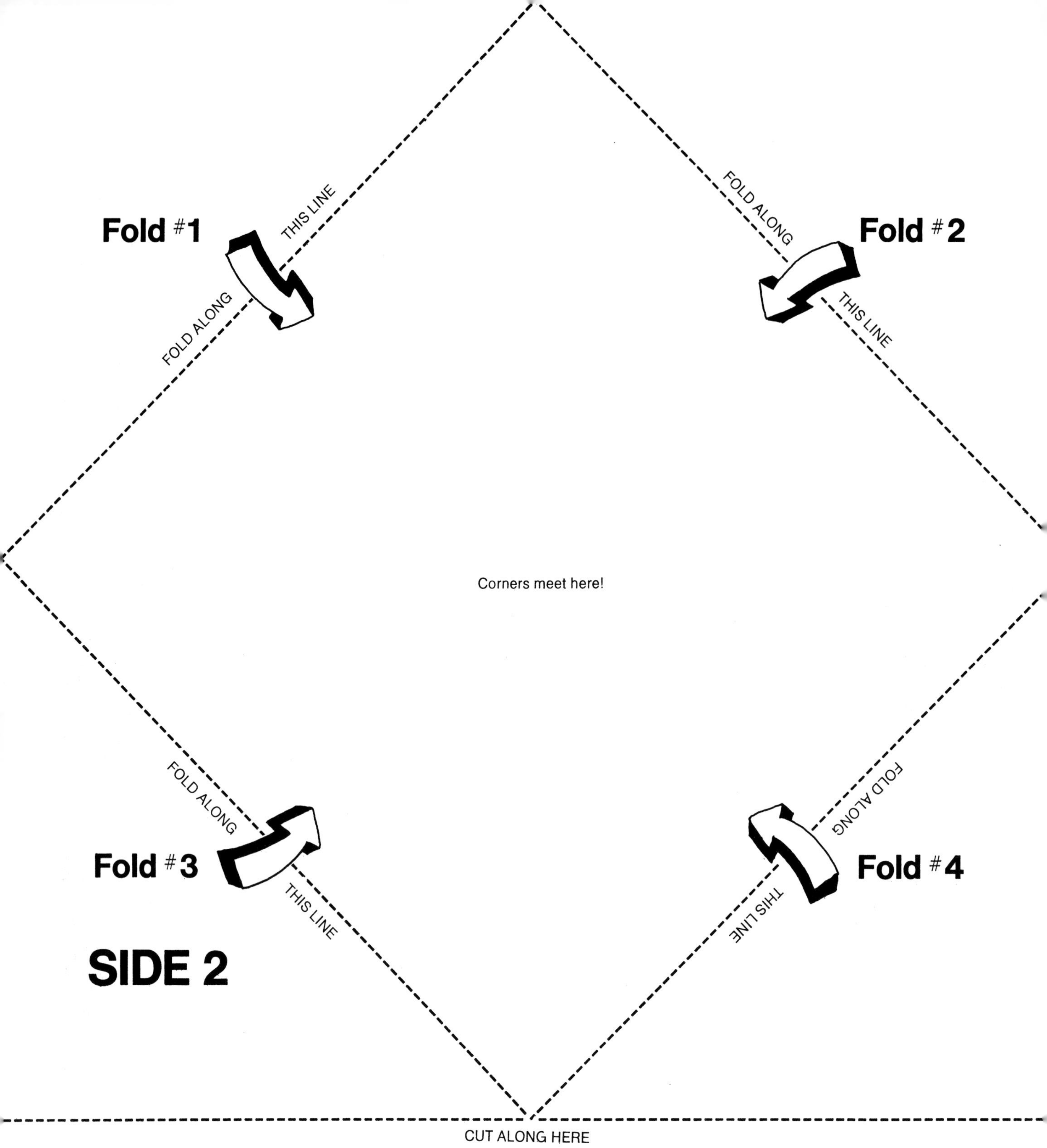

**Fold #1**

FOLD ALONG

THIS LINE

**Fold #2**

FOLD ALONG

THIS LINE

Corners meet here!

FOLD ALONG

**Fold #3**

THIS LINE

**Fold #4**

FOLD ALONG

THIS LINE

**SIDE 2**

CUT ALONG HERE

## HOW TO USE YOUR COOTIE CATCHER

**1.** Holding CATCHER so that VICTIM sees only *blank* interior portion, tell him you are "hunting for cooties."

**2.** Scratch VICTIM's scalp with CATCHER and, quickly shifting finger positions, show him the MAGICALLY REVEALED COOTIES!

**3.** Blow sharply on CATCHER and, simultaneously flicking wrist, switch fingers quickly and show VICTIM the empty CATCHER.

**4.** If you *failed to follow directions*, you probably fucked up several instructions ago. You can get a new square of paper and start again, drawing your own COOTIES in yourself, dumbbell.

Vol. XXIX, No. 17

BREAKS SCHOOL LIFE INTO COLORFUL NEWS

May 11, 1964

Quote of the Day

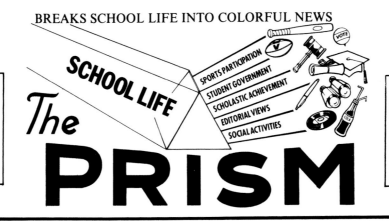

SCHOOL LIFE

*The* **PRISM**

SPORTS PARTICIPATION
STUDENT GOVERNMENT
SCHOLASTIC ACHIEVEMENT
EDITORIAL VIEWS
SOCIAL ACTIVITIES

*Jumpy Sez*

Don't attract de-tention!

# One-Way Stairs — Student Government in Action

by Chuck Farley

Self-government for the KHS student body means student independence *and* responsibility. That's why when Student Council members observed all the unnecessary crowding and hallway traffic jams they realized their responsibility to take legislative action and they were quick to act on the suggestion of Dr. Cornholt that certain staircases be designated down only and other staircases only up, for a trial period of one year. The change has been dramatic. Now, instead of enormous masses of students going up and down the stairs there are large crowds of students going down the stairs or up.

Student Council President Chuck Farley is proud of this latest KHS Student Government achievement. He states, "One-way stairs are an example of dynamic traffic control such as is being used in large high schools throughout our nation. Let me say now that I am very glad that Kefauver will not be among the last to find the time value of traffic direction."

This has been a landmark year for student self-government at KHS. Settling such potentially explosive issues as crowded halls and the prom dress debate without harmful controversy plus institution of a Student Court to handle all rules infractions involving a penalty of less than fifty Citizenship Demerit Points, not to mention placing a student suggestion box outside Room 211, have set real precedents at KHS. It's only one more way we've shown our teachers and parents that a new, mature generation of students have come to high school—a generation able to handle independence *and* responsibility.

There are some grumblers, however, who are saying that one-way stairs don't make any difference. It's hard to see how they can say that when so many students go up and down stairs every day. It's these people who think it's a laugh to go up a wrong staircase or down a wrong staircase during lunch or class periods when there isn't any traffic and no one's looking. But it should be remembered that one-way staircase rules have been passed by Student Council and so became school "laws" the moment they were passed and received advisor recommendation and administrative approval. And they carry a sixty-point Citizenship Demerit penalty for violation any time during the school day or when extracurricular activities are being held. So let's all pitch in and put an end to "Hallway Heck" at Kefauver High.

## New Stair Rules

*The new stair rules are: North and East Front stairs are up only except during lunch period and at 3:15 P.M. South Back and West Front stairs are down except before first bell and during homeroom. The Double Center stairs are up on the outside flights and down on the inside with direction reversed before and after assemblies, while the East Annex has only up stairways and the West Annex stairs are down unless there's athletic practice.*

# Wave of Vandalism Strikes KHS
## Culprit "Sick, not funny" Says Dr. Cornholt

C. Estes Kefauver High was the victim of its fifteenth major act of vandalism in as many weeks, *Prism* newssleuths were informed last Thursday afternoon in a hastily-arranged special assembly called by Principal Dr. Humphrey C. Cornholt. The vandalism, described to be the "work of a seriously troubled rule-breaker or rule-breakers unknown," was discovered in a downstairs boys' lavatory by Hall Monitor Carl D. Lepper immediately following an unannounced third period fire drill.

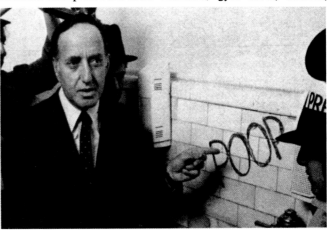

**Principal Cornholt says foot is himself.**

The vandalism, found stopping up a sink as Lepper routinely inspected the washroom for smoking materials, was accompanied by an obscenity on an adjoining wall. Upon closer inspection, custodial engineer Stanislav Dupa verified that the obscenity was written in the rule-breaker's own vandalism and subsequently tendered his resignation to Dr. Cornholt citing this and other vandalisms, including one in Mr. Dupa's lunchbox last month, as the reason.

The large four-letter work measuring approximately six by fourteen inches and the attendant vandalism in the washbasin are the most recent of a series of related incidents, according to highly-placed safety patrols. Since after the Christmas holidays, Kefauver High has been plagued by similar vandalisms including willfully defaced plaques, walls, wastebaskets, lockers, water fountains, behind hot radiators, bag lunches, gym shoes, mirrors, school bus gas tanks, teachers' lounge water coolers, cafeteria trays, art supply cabinets, and the new Student Council sponsored Student Suggestion Box which Class President Chuck Farley had hoped would be "a spur to good citizenship and an opportunity to air student views and gripes. Instead, the only thing that's gotten aired out is the Student Suggestion Box."

In the unprecedented lunch period special assembly, Dr. Cornholt declared that further

*continued on page 5*

# Kefauver "Einsteins" Battle TV Brain-Teasers Sail Through Sums, Stumped by Gumwad

Television was made a reality for two lucky seniors last Sunday morning at 5:45 A.M. when they challenged Our Lady of Pain in WPOX-TV's weekly "High School Knowledge Bowl." The "Knowledge Bowl" pits brains, not brawn, against each other for cash valued premiums and bulk awards, as well as a $100 scholarship to the college or university of their choice donated by the Van Husen Mobile Home Company to the annual champion.

Leonard Scrabbler, '64, and Belinda Heinke, '64, this year's salutatorian and valedictorian, respectfully, represented KHS last week against two Our Lady of Pain seniors. While the final score of 695 to 15 seemed somewhat lopsided, both Scrabbler, who was fourth runner-up in the state-wide Science Fair Exhibit Competition for his project "Fun With Breadmolds," and Heinke, who boasts Kefauver's coveted Current Events Beanie and this term's hotly-contested Perfect Attendance Citation, answered all questions politely and promptly, much of the blame for their disappointing showing being traced to Scrabbler's mistaking a gob of hardened chewing gum under his table for the answer buzzer.

The plucky Kangaruminators easily answered "States and Capitals," "Math on the March," and two out of three "Trailer Lore" brain-bogglers, also breezing through the special bonus "Spell That Color" and "Name That Shape" skull-scrappers, but lost valuable seconds and points as Scrabbler's fingers became increasingly cemented to the warmed-up old gumwad.

Incorrectly identifying the Canadian Soldier as the State Bird of Ohio, Heinke also mistakenly recognized" $\pi r^2$" as the formula for cubing a sphere and stumbled again as she gave the sign "$H_2O$" as the formula for the volume of a swimming pool.

Finally, the Kefauver Kangaputers fell irretrievably behind the Our Lady of Pain team when they named Booker T. Washington as the "first Negro father of his country" and a magnified frog heart as Australia.

Despite their disappointing totals, KHS eggheadliners spent many long hours of preparation quizzing each other on important dates, facts, names, and fractions which will come in handy on the "Knowledge Bowl of Real Life" if not the one of TV.

While the team failed to gain a rung on the ladder to the $100 scholarship, team coach Dwight Mannsburden looks forward to next year's contest when seniors Gilbert Scrabbler and Belinda Heinke will be freshmen at the college or university of their choice.

## Printing Error Keeps *Leaf and Squib* Out of Circulation

A printing mistake with a student drawing caused the KHS literary magazine *Leaf and Squib* to go off sale last week. *Squib* editor Forrest Swisher said Dr. Cornholt had pointed out what a mistake it was to print that drawing. Dr. Cornholt later had a helpful discussion with the *Squib* staff emphasizing that the body is the sacred temple of the spirit and art is the sacred temple of the mind and we should keep both neat and clean.

When asked what would be done with the leftover copies, Editor Swisher said that Dr. Cornholt had noticed some other errors too and so they couldn't just take out page 10 where the drawing with the mistake was. And Art Editor Faun Rosenberg suggested that all the issues be shoved or crammed someplace out of the way.

# TEEN CANTEEN OPEN

Youtherans, the Lutheran young people's organization, has opened a Teen Canteen in the basement of the Parkview Lutheran Church at the corner of North Cove and Upton Avenue. The new Canteen is nondenominational and teens of all faiths are welcome. Youtheran Coordinator Reverend Otis Peterson is very happy with the Canteen idea. He says, "Churches should get involved—tackling the real problems in this world. And the lack of a nice place to have fun is one very real problem for today's teens. After all," he says, "Christ was once a teenager, too."

Only six blocks from KHS, the Youtheran Teen Canteen will be a big plus for Kefauver students' recreation. It already has two bumper pool tables and it will be open until 9:30 P.M. every night. Many activities are planned including bumper pool tournaments, professional instruction in bumper pool, bumper pool teams, and city-wide bumper pool play-offs. The Youtherans hope to get a Coke machine soon and plan to hold a dance in the church gym this summer.

## LUNCHEON MENU
### Monday, May 11 through Friday, May 15

**MONDAY**
Choice of
Cheese Chow Mein
or
Individual Frank & Beans
Pickled Beets, Creamed Corn Niblets
Bun
Chocolate Dairy Drink
Butterscotch Pudding du Jour

**TUESDAY**
Choice of
Bologna Sandwich
or
Macarogni & Cheese
Sauerkraut, Chili Squares
Sweet Pickle
Slice White Bread, Pat Margarine
Neapolitan Ice Dessert Brick

**WEDNESDAY**
Choice of
Sloppy Joes
or
Knockwurst a la King
Pickled Egg, Stuffed Pepper
Grapefruit Ade
Soft Roll
Lime or Fish Jello

**THURSDAY**
Choice of
Olive Loaf
or
Spaghetti & Meatball
Cauliflower au Gratin, Succotash
Slice Date-Nut Bread & Cottage Cheese
V-8 Juice
Hot Prune Cobbler

**FRIDAY**
Choice of
Assorted Cold Luncheon Meats
or
Fish Sticks au Jus
Food Chowder & Oysterettes
Deviled Broccoli, Cream of Washroom Soup
Cranberry Ade
Graham Cracker w/Topping

## C. Estes Kefauver High School

**3301 Upton Ave.
Dacron, Ohio**

Published weekly except in the summer and during exam periods and school holidays or at Christmas.

### EDITORIAL STAFF

Editor in Chief .................................. Charles Farley
Associate Editor ....................,...... Herbert Weisenheimer
News Editor ......................... Woolworth Van Husen
Features Editor .............................. Wendy Dempler
Sports Editor .............................. Franklin Furter
Art Editor .................................. Faun Rosenberg
Photography Editor ......................... Forrest Swisher
Errands Editor ................................. Rufus Leaking

### BUSINESS STAFF

Business Manager ................................. Carl Lepper
Advertising Manager ............. Naomi Eggenschwiler
Typing Manager ......................... Ursula Wattersky

### ADVISORS

Editorial Copy ....................... Mrs. Evelyn Hampster
Business Management ................. Mrs. Olive Finch
Editorial Opinion ............... Dr. Humphrey Cornholt

## VANDALISM

What worse criminal is there than the school vandal? For almost any other crime there is a reason—no matter how bad a reason. But the school vandal doesn't need a reason. Even the Nazi Germans *thought* they were doing the right thing. But school vandals know that what they are doing isn't right. Everybody is harmed. And in one of the most important places, too—the American institution of free education for all. Education is free in this country but that doesn't mean it doesn't cost anything. And all the money spent cleaning up the disgusting vandalisms smeared around our school could be spent on valuable educational aids such as more language lab earphones, rear view projectors, and a new gym. But *that* doesn't stop the vandal. A vandal's the kind of person who invaded South Korea. He's like a senseless murderer who kills for no reason—murdering valuable new helps for learning that our school could have and, even worse, murdering the peacefulness and orderliness of our halls and classrooms which are so important to receiving a good education which we're all getting the chance to have. Some of us might not get into college. And that's murder.

## ONE-WAY STAIRS

And what about those people who disregard the "rules of the road" on our one-way staircases? Aren't they just about the same as school vandals? After all, they are vandalizing everyone's valuable time by causing unnecessary crowding and hallway traffic jams when, in fact, it was unnecessary crowding and hallway traffic jams which caused the Student Council (with a helpful suggestion by Dr. Cornholt) to pass the legislation which gives us one-way staircases in the first place. Everyone should remember that this is only a trial period and if we don't give the one-way stairs a fair trial period then how will Dr. Cornholt know whether to suggest that the Student Council make one-way stairs permanent forever or suggest that we go back to the two-way stairs we had in the past? Why all the harmful controversy?

## COMPROMISE

Speaking of harmful controversy, let's not forget that there's one most important basic principle which rests at the foundations of the American Way of Life—*compromise*. And we can find a great lesson in compromise right here in our school this spring. Remember the heated debate over "Formal Dress for the Senior Prom"? Some students felt that requiring formal wear put a strain on the budgets of students from less fortunate families. While other students felt that Kefauver High should maintain its important traditions. There were good arguments on both sides, but harmful controversy was avoided when Student Council President "Chuck" Farley proposed that required formal dress continue but that all corsages and boutonnieres be identical and moderately priced. Thus, less fortunate students were partly spared a large expense. And the mums looked beautiful, too. That's the kind of thinking we need more of, and that's the kind of thinking we should all apply to the one-way stairs.

## SCHOOL SPIRIT

But, important as compromise is, there are some places where there's no room for it. School Spirit is one of those places. And School Spirit is exactly the place where most of us compromise. "Not enough School Spirit at KHS?!! How can that be said," you may say, "when almost every sports event is packed with cheering students and nearly every victory or loss seems to be almost a life or death matter for most of our students?!" But real School Spirit is more than cheering our many teams and being proud of and loyal to Kefauver High. Real School Spirit is obeying all the rules.
—The Editor

# Class Gift Selected

Members of the Kefauver High Class of '64 have decided to go together with the Class of '65 to present one large class gift to the high school. The officers of the two classes gathered and after a discussion they decided to donate a Senior Drinking Fountain to be installed in the West Hall foyer. The drinking fountain will bear an inscription reading "Gift of the Classes of 1964 and 1965." Only seniors will be permitted to drink from it. Thus, the class officers felt, not only would KHS seniors be provided with another welcome drinking fountain but Kefauver would also acquire an important continuing tradition to be passed down through the years, helping to add prestige and pride to the position of Senior student.

Past class gifts have been

New Senior Drinking Fountain will show modern style.

many. The Class of 1955 went together with the Class of 1956 to donate brass plaques inscribed with the Lord's Prayer for every classroom. The Class of 1957 donated the Senior Seal in the floor of the main East Vestibule and which it is a continuing KHS tradition that only seniors can walk on. The Class of 1959 gave us our four-foot-high cement statue of Jumpy which stands in front of the football practice field. The Class of 1960 donated a bench. The Classes of 1961 and 1962 went together to have all the Lord's Prayer plaques removed. And the Class of 1963 bought the orange and turquoise window shades in the Senior Study Hall.

## *Jumpy Sez*

Only twenty-six days left to study for final examinations!

# "Camelot" Senior Prom "Joust Delightful"

The lore and legend of King Arthur's Round Table was made a reality for a gymful of lucky lords and their ladies last weekend as the Class of '64's Kanga-Krusaders stormed the gym for their "much-heralded" Class of 1964 Senior Prom!

Starting off with a "Proclamation of Fun" from "Sir Dancelot" (a thinly-disguised well-known Health and Drivers Ed teacher in shining armor), followed by a grand procession under the Pavilion of Crepe Paper and a stop at the Round Table of Refreshments, the evening was topped off with another remarkable demonstration of the Charleston by Mr. Dwight Mannsburden and Mrs. Noreen Fitzerman.

When the chimes of midnight struck, the enchanted scene, a fantasy of Arthurian castles, parapets, and balloon-bedecked basketball hoops, was "turned back into a pumpkin" as chivalrous Kanga-Rollickers plucked souvenirs of the gala event for their fair damsels, including gaily-decorated poster-paint "tapestries" and the Holy Hawaiian Punch Grail which Dr. Cornholt would like returned immediately along with the band's accordian and he isn't kidding.

The after-party in the parents of Woolworth Van Husen III's very gracious and elegant wood-paneled rumpus room was an added "boon" as the feudal fun-seekers toasted the future with their favorite chips 'n' dips.

All in all, the Class of '64 agreed that the evening was a great succeess, and despite the unbecoming behavior of a certain small element of the guests and the unfortunate car accident resulting in the death of six graduating seniors and their dates, a good time was had by most.

## Student Court Means Student Independence AND Student Responsibility

Our new Student Court moved into gear last Tuesday with its first case under the new rules allowing students who've violated a rule which carries a penalty of fifty Citizenship Demerit Points or less their choice between going to the Dean's Office or being tried by a Student Court of their peer group.

The institution of a Student Court is a landmark precedent in the annals of KHS student self-government, allowing students themselves to set up and participate in one of the basic foundations of justice and democracy in our nation, which is our national judicial system. Student Council elected Student Council President Chuck Farley to be this year's judge. Dr. Cornholt appointed Senior Carl Lepper as Student Prosecutor and Winky Dempler as Court Stenographer. And Hall Monitors have promised to supply a Sergeant at Arms for each trial. Student Court trials will be held during sixth period study hall. Students being tried can pick any other student their age as their "lawyer," and either side may call any student witness who isn't in class that period.

The first case in a Student Court trial got started when Hall Monitor Naomi Eggenschwiler observed junior Patty Jo Shinski wearing a skirt with length that fell above the knees. Naomi reported this violation of the KHS dress code to Hall Monitor sponsor Miss Armbruster who ordered Patty Jo to come to her office where she was given the "carpet kneeling" test. Patty Jo's skirt did not touch the carpet when she was in a kneeling position as KHS dress code requires, but since the skirt was less than two-and-three-quarters inches above the carpet (and therefore the penalty for wearing it was forty Citizenship Demerit Points instead of eighty, which it would have been if the skirt had been more than two-and-three-quarters inches above the carpet), Miss Armbruster gave Patty Jo a choice between seeing the Girl's Dean, who is Miss Armbruster, or being tried in Student Court and sent Patty Jo home to change her skirt so that she was only counted two-and-a-third periods absent without an excuse instead of being sent home for the entire day. When the trial began, Student Prosecutor Carl Lepper called Sergeant at Arms Naomi Eggenschwiler to testify that Patty Jo Shinski had been wearing the skirt which he had as evidence in the Court because Miss Armbruster made Patty Jo bring it back to school with her after she went home to change. Naomi said that Patty Jo had been wearing the short skirt. Then Carl called Pinky Albright as a witness and Pinky said that Naomi was always very honest and she'd seen Patty Jo wearing that skirt before anyway. When it was the defense's turn, Patty Jo pleaded that she had accidentally hiked the skirt up too high when she was tucking her blouse in in the girls' washroom. Student Judge Chuck Farley decided that Patty Jo should get forty Citizenship Demerit Points.

**Student Court—does it mean Independence, or Responsibility?**

Class of '54 had just returned from Senior Trip to Washington, D.C. Student Council was debating new "keep-left" hallway passing period regulations; Principal Howard M. Conrad suggested a two-semester trial period. Class play, *Romeo and Juliet*, debuted to rave reviews. Prom theme was "Castles in Spain." North Lawn's Senior Elm Tree was planted as Class Gift. *Prism* editorial deplored broken windows, asked student cooperation in keep-left passing periods. Y-Teens opened special "Young People's Lounge" at West Dacron Branch YMCA. Homecoming Queen Mary Jo Hall won 2nd place in Friendly Order of Opossums Talent Contest. Veterans of Foreign Wars volunteers were helping School Librarian Miss Violet Coolidge cart away old sets of John Dos Passos novels. Student Deportment Tribunal was instituted to assist in disciplining student deportment violations. Dispute over Class Rings ended in a compromise when Class President Ernie Simpkis suggested that gold plating be kept but rings should be offered in only one style to spare expense for students with modest means. "Inquiring Kangaroo" asked students how they felt about new passing period regulations. KHS baseball team lost close contest to Warren G. Harding 15 to 0. Football Awards Dinner saw Senior Q.B. receive league-wide kudos for "Most Yardage Gained on a Statue of Liberty Play." And Ballroom Dance team scored first in city.

## Patriotic Group Helps Annual Library Cleanup

After a whole school year of checking out books and having them returned (sometimes late with a *fine!*), our busy school library gets pretty confused! And now's the time to be putting everything in order: neat and ready for next fall's whole new class of Kefauveroos and 'Rettes and all the returning students who'll be coming back. So, last week, it was time for the annual library cleanup.

This year, members of the Flugencia Batista Chapter of the Christian Anti-Communist Crusade volunteered to help school Librarian Violet Coolidge straighten things out.

There's only so much room in a library and Miss Coolidge and her volunteers have been really busy deciding what books will serve all Kefauver students best. A choice has to be made between important books which help us in our school work such as *Colliers Encyclopedia* and other books which there may not be room for. As Miss Coolidge says, "Shelf space is just like space in our minds."

When spring cleaning was done Miss Coolidge and her helpers had made room for a second complete set of bound *National Geographics* plus extra copies of *I Saw Poland Betrayed*, *The Invisible Government*, and *Masters of Deceit*. But it looks like there won't be room for the old Upton Sinclair books, back issues of *Saturday Review*, or a subscription to the *Sunday New York Times* next year.

# KANGARUMORS

### by Fizzie

Everybody's pouch is flapping with this week's 'Roo "tails" about . . . the mum smell at Senior Prom . . . Emily Praeger's nine pound, six ounce tonsils . . . school nurse giving "French" 1,000,000 units of penicillin for a case of the "hives". . . page ten in the latest *Leaf and Squib* . . . the Senior Drinking Fountain tradition . . . all the mud in the Mobile Home Bowl . . . hockey in April . . . and *most of all*, the Mad You-Know-Whater!!!!! . . .

# KHS Student Places High in Miss Teenage Dacron Contest

The pride of Kefauver High was on display last Wednesday night when KHS senior Amana Peppridge (this year's Homecoming Queen and Kangarooters Kaptain) won third runner-up in the Miss Teenage Dacron Contest. Amana was awarded a beautiful green Fold-Flush Travel Tent complete with screened windows.

Every year the Miss Teenage Dacron Contest is held to select the best rounded teenage girl in Dacron. The winner goes on to participate in the Miss Teenage Silage County Contest at the County Fair next fall. Entrants are judged on the basis of charm, deportment, tidy appearance, and talents. Also, each contestant must give an original speech on the subject, "Why I Want to Be Miss Teenage Da-

cron." Amana Peppridge recited Edgar Allen Poe's poem "The Raven" as her talent contribution and titled her speech, "My Reasons for Wanting to Be Miss Dacron Are Twofold—First, to Someday Proudly Represent Dacron, Ohio, in the Miss Teenage Midwest Contest in Indianapolis. And, Second, to Meet New People in All Walks of Life."

The title of Miss Teenage Dacron went this year to Annette Velocipeda, Junior at Our Lady of Pain, who won a completely furnished house trailer and a $400 scholarship to the college of her choice. First runner-up went to Andrea Pettibone of Warren G. Harding High, while second was captured by Constance Nowakowski from Prendergast.

**KHS Senior Amana Peppridge recites Edgar Allen Poe's "The Raven" during Talent Test in Miss Teenage Dacron Contest held at the Mobile Home Bowl Auditorium.**

# 'Roo Ribs

**by "Wing-Ding" Weisenheimer**

Well, it's baseball season and our team's out there fanning themselves even though it isn't very hot yet. . . . Boy, it must be the reason they call us Kangaroos is we're always **down under!** . . . What about these one-way stairs, huh? . . . You know what the mixed-up freshman did when he had to go back and forth between floors? **He justed "staired" one way and then the other!** . . . But I've got a better idea —how about **one-way grades!** . . . **Up** only!!! . . . I'm not saying anything bad about our baseball team but it smells to me like the **M.C.** has been visiting their box scores! . . . **Mum's** the word about the Senior Prom, but they don't call it **punch** for nothing! . . . Sure are a lot of homeroom bulletins lately . . . don't know about you, but I'm getting **bulletin bored!** . . . Spring issue of the **Leaf and Squib**—copies sure went **quick** if you get what I mean . . . And if you do you ought to get a look at page ten . . . if the Hall Monitors don't get it first! . . . "Preggers" is wondering who gave her "tonsilitis." . . . Don't

look at me! . . . What's huge and orange and turquoise and hasn't won a game all year? . . . **Moby Kangaroo!** . . . I thought you had to be twenty-one to be a tavern keeper in Ohio but ya' see "Psycho" **behind bars** all the time! . . . Question: How can you tell when the **M.C.** has gotten into the cafeteria food? . . . Answer: **You can't!!!** . . . Knock, knock. . . . Who's there? . . . Jumpy. . . . Jumpy who? . . . **Did Jumpy the garbage yet**?! . . . Seen our gym towels lately? . . . Either the laundry service is on strike or Zippy fades when wet! . . . Why'd the Kangaroo put on a pair of nylons? . . . He wanted to have a **sock hop**! . . . Oooh, that one was straight from the **M.C.** . . . And, as the ole **M.C.** always says—gotta **go** now! . . . Don't "pull any pouches" and see ya next week!!!

**Jumpy:** What time is it when the big hand is on "12" and the little hand is between the "12" and the "1"?
**Jumpy Jr.:** Lunchtime!

**Jumpy:** What's red and white and grey all over?
**Jumpy Jr.:** Kambell's Kream of Kangaroo Soup!

# As We Go to Press

Emily May Praeger has been admitted to the Florence Hazelwitt Foundling's Home to have her tonsils removed. She'll be home in about a month. . . . Till then, get well soon cards can be sent care of Hazelwitt Home, 4800 Sylvania Ave. . . .

The new Senior Drinking Fountain tradition, a KHS traditional senior privilege, will begin promptly at 3:00 P.M. Wednesday, May 13. . . .

Date for the long-awaited city-wide Football Awards Banquet has been set for next Saturday, May 16, now that the bugs which plagued our Mixed Chorus' performance at the Roads Commissioner's Convention have been worked out of the new Mobile Home Bowl Banquet Arena. . . . 'Roo Grid Greats look like hot contenders for "Most Improved Team" again this year.

---

## Jumpy Sez

Don't get "up-set" on a Down staircase!

---

# Vandalism

*continued*

vandalisms would "not be tolerated, even if it means boarding up all lavatories or requiring a buddy system for their continued use."

Dr. Cornholt went on to stress the importance of students' cooperation in identifying the "criminally delinquent" individual or individuals, and announced the posting on all bulletin boards of 500 Good Citizenship Credits to any student for information leading to his capture and expulsion. A number of suspects have already been sent to the Principal's Office for questioning while Hall Monitors and Lavatory Patrols have been doubled as a purely precautionary measure. In addition, Principal Cornholt remarked, he has named a number of "Special Anti-Vandalism Auxiliaries" from the seventh and eighth grades empowered to make "Good Citizenship Arrests" and who are temporarily excused from the General Deportment Rules against unnecessary tattling and snitching on fellow pupils.

"These are stern measures," Dr. Cornholt remarked, "but the situation is getting out of hand, and if the so-called 'Mad Vandal' does not report to the

*continued*

## Vandalism
*continued*

office by next Thursday, no final report cards will be given out, and Eskimo Pie and chocolate milk privileges will be denied *all* students, guilty and innocent alike." Dr. Cornholt also said recess periods might be seriously curtailed.

Since early in the term, Dr. Cornholt told the entire student body as they settled down to listen attentively in the gym, the rule-breaker or "Mad Vandal" as he is known to some students has made many locations within the building and grounds unfit for healthful classroom activities, disrupting regular routines and causing upset among the girls.

The "Mad Vandal" has already gained the unwelcomed attention of the *Dacron Daily Telegraph* in a series of feature articles and editorials, the last of which, entitled "Outrage Stalks the Halls," was read on television station WPOX.

Past vandalisms on school property, while displaying no particular pattern, are more difficult to find the perpetrator of because they often occur during fire drills, school assemblies, mass pep rallies, or after school hours. The first vandalism, which was discovered floating in the school swimming pool by Senior Robert Baxter, Jr., while breaststroking against St. Vitus, and which may have contributed to Baxter's poor time, was estimated to have been committed while most students were attending Booster Day Activities in the gym. During the assembly, a delegation from the Varsity Club presented Dr. Cornholt with the annual "Principal of the Year" award after calling him away from his regular duties.

Dr. Cornholt has already assured concerned parents, PTA members, and School Board Officials that while vandalisms of such seriousness had never before happened at Kefauver, Dr. Cornholt was not going to sit idly by while "some ·sick, twisted youth or youths foul my many unsmudged years as an educator. These vandalisms are even becoming a hazard to the orderly flow of hall traffic, and I think it's time for somebody to put their foot down. That foot is me."

# Sr. Trippers Bus to Big Apple
# Good Time Had by All

The glamour and glitter of Manhattan, New York, was made a reality for six lucky Kangaroamers a few weekends ago when Suzi Fitzerman, Gilbert Scrabbler, Woolworth Van Husen III, Patricia Ann Albright, Wendy Ann Dempler, Leonard Weisenheimer, and Senior Trip Sponsor Mr. Duane Postum enjoyed a memorable and unforgettable weekend in one of America's largest and most exciting metropolises.

"I never thought the buildings were so tall!" remarked Suzi Fitzerman, '64. "Now I know why they call them 'skyscrapers'!"

"And with all the dog vandalisms on the sidewalks," added Leonard Weisenheimer, "they should have built a few footscrapers, too."

Departing from the Downtown Dacron Greyhound Bus Terminal, Ohio's junior ambassadors of fun motored almost straight through, stopping only for a short sight-seeing break while the bus fixed a flat in very interesting Buffalo, New York. "I never knew it took so long to change one of those tires," exclaimed Suzi Fitzerman, '64.

When the globe-hoppers checked into their rooms at the very famous and economical Penn-Garden Hotel, located in the heart of New York's famous street district, they went immediately to the Empire State Building ("or *Entire* State Building!" adds Leonard Weisenheimer, '64), stopping off only for a few minutes at the seventy-ninth floor so that ears could "unpop" and Gilbert Scrabbler, '64, could get a Kleenex for a bad nosebleed.

Traveling around the city, the Seniors learned many new and interesting things, including the surprising fact that a taxi ride from Forty-second Street and Seventh Avenue to Times Square cost a whopping $15!

Sadder but wiser, the travelers soaked up other remarkable sights, sounds, and smells, including the very interesting Ripley's *Believe It or Not* exhibit featuring a very interesting miniature log cabin made completely out of Lincoln head pennies, the angry rat-tat-tat-tat-tat of noisy jackhammers, and the many dog vandalisms on the sidewalks. ("Instead of 'Curb your dog,' the signs should read, 'Oh, forget it,'" commented Leonard Weisenheimer, '64.)

The high point of the trip was, of course, the 1964 World's Fair held at Flushing Meadows, New York. There they inhaled many heady sights and sounds such as the Pepsi Cola Pavilion, with its many wonderful and interesting Disney-animated mechanical foreigners who sang "It's a Small World After All" over and over and over again. ("I never knew anybody could sing the same song so many times," reported Kangarambler Wendy Ann Dempler, "not even robots. The mechanical sidewalk broke down and we had to listen to it over and over again. Gilbert counted we listened to it 302 times until he lost count on account of his real bad nosebleed. It was kind of creepy.")

Other remarkable sights and views they saw were the GE Carousel of Progress, which gave a very interesting lesson on important breakthroughs on advanced refrigerator technology. Also, the Formica House, made entirely of Formica, and the Court of the Universe, where tired toes dabbled in the Fountain of the Planets until somebody yelled at us.

Back at the hotel, Mr. Postum found that the bill for the weekend included plumbing bills for certain plumbing that was damaged from an unidentified cherry bomb in the pipes and everybody arrived back Sunday night, tired but happy that they had peeled the core of the "Big Apple" and had found many juicy stories as well as the pits.

# Court Kangaroos Lose St. Vitus Trial

### by Charles Ulmer Farley

When the Kefauver varsity hoopsters faced the St. Vitus Academy netmen Saturday, May 2, many thought the Kangaroo roundballers would be blown out of the almost fully-repaired Mobile Home Bowl Arena by the Penguin cagers. Not so! Bob Baxter, Jr., playing the pivot for the Orange and Turquoise sneakermen, won a rare center tap to open the initial stanza, and, seconds later, Kefavorite guard Madison Avenue "Zippy" Jones faked his man into tripping over one of the several remaining uneven spots on the Arena floor. Swish! The 'Roo backcourt specialist's quick turnaround jump shot dented the twines, and the upset-minded Marsupial parqueteers found themselves holding their first lead of the season!

Time was not on the side of the ill-starred C. Estes courtesans, however, as John "Johnny Boy" Vigilanti, stalwart for-ward for the St. Vitus bucketmen, laid in the equalizer, and the Penguin dribblers went on to defeat our 'Roo-bounders by the quite convincing margin of 73-17.

High scorer for the KHS hardwoodmen, who once again sorely missed the services of the late Howard Lewis Havermeyer, was Vince "French" Lambretta, who dropped in a season-high total of seven points for the Kefauverster courtiers.

Next Saturday, Coach Duane "Instant" Postum's winless sweatmen will again take to the still-warped floor of the Mobile Home Bowl Arena, where they'll play host to the Fender Benders of Tucker Technical High School. The game will mark the end of the campaign for both fives—a campaign delayed for more than two months by repairs to Dacron's magnificent, but seemingly jinxed, new sports facility.

## Sharp-shoe-ters Take Aim at Harding; Hyenas Laugh Them Off

### by Charles Ulmer Farley

When the Kefauver varsity hockey team faced the Warren G. Harding High School icemen last April 27, many thought the Kangaroo puck passers would be blown out of the almost fully-repaired Mobile Home Bowl Arena by the Hyena skatemen. Not so! Robert "Flinch" Baxter, centering the first line for the Orange and Turquoise padclads, won a rare face-off to open the initial stanza, and, seconds later, Kefavorite right wing Vincent Lambretta was bearing down on Lorne Moaire, stalwart Canadian-born netminder for the Harding frigidaires. Whack! The 'Roo goalprospector uncorked a mighty slap shot that ricocheted off a broken pipe sticking up through the playing surface and caught the corner of the Hyena icecrushers' net, and the upset-minded Marsupial rubberchasers found themselves holding their first lead of the season! Time was not on the side of the hapless C. Estes rinky-dinks, however, as Pouchster backliner Bruno "Lurch" Grozniak inadvertently tied the contest by shooting the disk into his own cage, and the Harding blade stars went on to defeat the Freezer-'Roos by the quite convincing margin of 23-2.

A bright spot for the KHS puckers, who once again sorely missed the services of the late Howard Lewis Havermeyer, was the play of "French" Lambretta, whose third-period tally enabled him to register the first two-goal cap trick of his Kefauverster spear-carrier career.

Tuesday, the winless rink rats will again take to the still-mushy ice of the Mobile Home Bowl Arena, where they'll play host to the Skating Penguins of St. Vitus Academy for Boys. The game will mark the end of the campaign for both sixes—a campaign delayed for more than two months by repairs to Dacron's magnificent, but seemingly hexed, new sports facility.

# 'Roo Fingermen Outpeck Wingnuts

Inspired by the unexpected presence of Cheerleader Captain Amana Swansdown Peppridge and her three deputy Kangarooters, Winky Dempler, Pinky Albright, and Twinky Croup (not to mention Jumpy, the Kefauver Kangaroo, who was attending her first typing bee ever), our varsity spacebar-risters fingered their way April 30, in Homeroom 6, to an easy victory over the badly outclassed Wingnut carriage drivers of Tucker Tech.

The contest stayed close through the early tab-setting and tab-clearing events, but then Pouchster bell-ringer Angela DeMohrning pulled off a brilliant ribbon reverse, and, when Clatteroo Rufus Leaking followed with two excellent shift locks to widen the Hunt-and-Peckers, margin to twelve big points, the typewriting was on the wall as far as the Tucker lettermen were concerned.

And so the regular season ends for Coach Mrs. Olive Finch's Longtail back-spacers, who must now sit back and wait for what most regard as a certain bid to participate in the State Championship Heptagonal Typing Bee in Youngstown in early June.

"A decision on whether or not to attend the Heps, assuming our Magic Marginiers are invited, will depend on the exam schedules of the individual typing team members," said Dr. Cornholt, who was among the enthusiastic spectators as the 'Roo key-tappers pounded the Fender Benders. "It's unfortunate the State Bee coincides with the close of our school year, but it does, and, after all, academics, not athletics, is C. Estes Kefauver High School's first priority."

Taking a slight edge off the Marsupial ribbon-changers' victory smiles was another of those unhappy instances of vandalism that have plagued our school in recent months. Dr. Cornholt, who discovered the pile of defacement himself upon his early arrival in Homeroom 6, termed the matter a "terrible, asinine waste."

# News From Mobile Home Bowl Brings Excitement Here

May 4th brought a good deal of excitement to Dacron city schools, not to mention numerous sighs of relief.

Mr. Fausto X. Brocolli, foreman of the Mobile Home Bowl Arena repair crew (and father of KHS senior Dominic Brocolli) informed School Superintendent Doggerty's office with the welcome news that the last leak in the plumbing beneath the Arena floor will soon be plugged. When the leak is completed, Mr. Brocolli explained, there should no longer be wet mushy areas whenever the ice surface is put down, and work can shortly begin on a new basketball court for tournament play without fears that the boards will warp as soon as they're put in place.

Construction on Dacron's magnificent new Mobile Home Bowl Sports and Entertainment complex started just three years ago on riverfront landfill property donated by the Mobile Home Manufacturers Association and filled in by the City Sanitary Engineers Landfill Division. Now almost complete, the Mobile Home Bowl will serve Dacron well in many capacities, not the least of which is as a location for High School hockey competition and play-offs, tournaments, and banquets of all kinds.

School Superintendent Philo M. Doggerty congratulated Mr. Brocolli and the entire Siciliano Construction Company whose work on the Mobile Home Bowl is now drawing to a close. Mr. Doggerty said that by next year the Dacron Public Schools should be able to run their winter sports activities on a better scheduled footing and voiced hope that Dacron School teams would achieve better state-wide standings when top athletes did not have to divide their spring training efforts among hockey, basketball, swimming, tennis, track, and baseball.

# Kangaroo Bowl-a-Dromedaries Roll Over Championship Hump

As Jumpy, the Kangaroo (who, of course, is really a kangaroo suit with Suzi Fitzerman inside) hopped for joy and the C. Estesettes elatedly twirled their batons, the varsity bowling team rolled over the Ezra Taft Benson Bobcat lanemen last Thursday afternoon in the Bowl-a-Drome to clinch their first Greater Dacron Ten-Pin League Championship.

Outstanding performances for Coach Miss Marilyn Armbruster's longtail alley cats were turned in by Captain Herbert Leonard "Wing-Ding" Weisenheimer, who rolled not one, but *two* over-200 games for our pin woodsmen, and by Dominic "DOM" Brocolli, who came through with three straight strikes to defeat his Benson guttersnipe opponent by a single point.

As Weisenheimer entered the tenth frame of his second win —the game that actually nailed down the 13-5 victory for the Orange and Turquoise bowly-rollers—the entire Kefauver student body, which had been excused early from classes so it could attend the event, rose to its collective feet and gave the Bowl-a-roo team leader a thundering standing ovation.

And here's an ironic "laner note": Wing-Ding had not even been scheduled to start the game that eventually proved to be the clincher for our frame-throwers! Originally, Emily May Praeger was to have had that honor, but her unexpected case of tonsilitis cost the unlucky Pouchster pin-wizardess her chance for alley immortality.

# "From the Pouch"

Views on Sport by Franklin George Furter

## Howard Lewis Havermeyer, 1947-1963

In taking an overall view of the performance of this year's athletic teams, not to mention the Class of '64's recent showing on the Scholastic Aptitude Tests, we are sure you will agree that our loss of Howard Lewis Havermeyer, fatally tackled by leukemia just as he appeared ready to romp into the end zone of a brilliant high school career, was a most tragic event indeed.

Not all of us knew Howard well, due primarily to his shy nature and his frequent absence due to illness. But he always had a ready smile for every classmate, and who knows to what dizzy heights he might have risen on the playing field or in the classroom, if Death had not hip-checked him into the boards just as he appeared ready to break in alone on the goal?

We're assured that Howard's leadership and ability would have made him a success in any endeavor, and feel it is now up to the rest of us to pick up the ball and follow the example he never had the chance to set.

# Girls' Sports

by Naomi Eggenschwiler

The Babe Didrikson Zaharias Club has chosen May 26 for the annual intra-mural Aqua-Hockey Nite, which will be held in the shallow end of the Dacron Municipal Swimming Pool. The bus will leave from the front of the Girls' gym promptly at 4:00 P.M., and those wishing to rent swim fins or field hockey sticks should check in with Club Sergeant at Arms Francine Paluka no later than 3:30 P.M.

The Girls' sophomore wrestling team traveled across town to Ezra Taft Benson High last May 1, and the Kangaroo second-year grapplerettes lost to the Battling Bobkittens by the rather lopsided score of 37-6. The only non-loser for the Pouchsterix canvasbacks was junior Laurie "Big" Riggs, who fought her Benson soph matwoman opponent to a dead heat.

The annual junior "Jumpy" tryouts are being planned and will commence in the near future. All those who wish to take a crack at being Kefauver High's lovable kangaroo mascot for 1964-1965 should get in touch with Cheerleader Captain Amana "Fridge" Peppridge no later than May 15.

# Splasharoos Drowned by Boss Prendergast

This year's varsity swimming team has not met with overwhelming success, and the Kangaroos' May 4 meet against the Lampreys of Boss Prendergast High School, despite the Pouchmen's fierce desire for victory, did not prove an exception, as the $H_2O$'sters paddled home on the short end of a 76-9 tally.

Kefauver poolshark Bob "Flinch" Baxter did cause some early excitement for the visiting Orange and Turquoise trunksters, splashing to a third place in the 200-yard individual medley after Prendergast wetback Gerber Toddlermeale was disqualified for making two false starts. But from there on it was more sink than swim for the C. Estes Aquanaughts, with Bruno Grozniak, in the 440-yard freestyle, being the only Splasharoo to salvage even so much as a fourth place finish for the unfortunate chlorinemen, who, forced once again to take to the pool without the late Howard Lewis Havermeyer, suffered their thirty-fifth consecutive tank defeat.

# "*Leaf & Squib*"

VOL Ⅱ · Number 2 · Spring · 1964

Our Cover:  "GROUNDED"
an original linoleum cut by Faun Rosenberg.


After consultation with our Faculty Sponsor,
Miss Hampster, we, this year's editors of the
"Leaf and Squib," decided to break with tradition
and make our cover an original work of art by
Faun Rosenberg, our Art Editor, rather than the
old traditional "leaf and squib" which now appears
on our title page.

# TABLE OF CONTENTS

STAFF

Editors in Chief.............Forrest Lawford Swisher, Faun Rosenberg

Art Editor...................................Faun Rosenberg

Prose and Poetry Editor..........................F.L. Swisher

Assistant Art Editor.............................Suzi Fitzerman

Assistant Editor................................Lawrence Kroger

Contributing Artist................................M.A. Jones

# the identity factory

By Faun Rosenberg

```
THEY
say to you conform with
their minds like airconditioned
parkinglots scream don't Don't DON'T
like the razorsharp edge of the cookiecutter
massproducing plastic
conformists with crabgrass hearts and ninetofive
buttondown greyflannel souls
pin butterflies like dead stamps in the
orderly albums of their martini
drinking empty twocar lives THEY
hurt Hurt HURT everyone
who isn't too blind to see the colors
of the feet of the pigeons in the park


THEY
pray to their whitewash God
and powermow the flowers every
phony sunday before monday ratrace traffic
boobtube hypnotized ears deaf to the
pain Pain PAIN of the broken glass
street brick beard stubble winos in the
doorways by their add hot water and serve
mankind religion of lies Lies LIES
and the carousel wooden horses song and the tears
first love must cry every rebellious
Spring.
```

# The Color of Freedom

By Forrest L. Swisher

Holy Gosh!  What time was it anyway, I wondered.
The darned alarm hadn't gone off again!  And I was
going to be late for class.  I got dressed, grabbed
my books, dashed out the door, and ran for the bus.
Just made it!  Now for a typical day, I thought.

Out of breath, I took the first seat I could
find.  Suddenly, a harsh, deep voice said loudly,
"Yo' git yo'self to de back ob dis here bus, whigger
boy!"  Wildly confused, I looked around me.  Everyone on this bus was Negro, except for one old man
sitting right at the back.  And the biggest Negro
was beside me, his white teeth bared in an ugly
sneer of racism!

"Wh--wh--what?" I stammered, stunned and
insulted.

page two

"Yo' all better jes' move yo' white self right
now, whigger. We all don't take kindly to yo' in-
ferior kind!" my colored seat mate hissed viciously.


I got up and staggered to the back of the bus,
sitting down beside the old white man. "Take it
easy, son. Don't be a troublemaker," he whispered
to me quietly. "Someday we'll all be equal, just
wait and see."


"Good Gosh!" I thought. "So this is what it's
like to be a member of a minority group!" I could
feel the hate, the ignorance, and prejudice in the
air of the bus like an odor. A musky, acidic odor
of fear and anger you could almost feel. I was
sweating, I realized, and part of that odor was me!
I kept my eyes lowered in shame until the bus rum-
bled and shuddered to my stop. I ran out the door,
with cries of, "Dirty whigger!" behind me.


Hardly knowing where I was, but remembering
I was late, I sprinted up the school steps. But
when I reached the doors, I realized that an
enormous Negro in a police uniform was standing
in front of them, his arms folded. He was carrying
a gun. Beside him, on a leash, were the biggest
police dogs I'd ever seen. Like him, they were
snarling and salivating. His face, like theirs,
was a mask of prejudice.


"Jes' where you all think you all goin', l'il
white boy?" was all he said. By now, I was afraid,
but I was angry, too.


"I have a right to go to school!" I shouted.
"I'm an American citizen! I've lived in this town
all my life! How can a person be so blind as to
judge another by the color of his skin?" I de-
manded. "After all, this is 1964!"


He just laughed a bitter, cynical laugh of
contempt. "You all are a pretty uppity little
whigger, ain't you?" he sneered. "Maybe I unleash
these here guard dogs, an' teach you yo' place!"


I was surrounded, all of a sudden. Dark-
skinned teenagers, men and women, the whole town
were lining the sidewalk to the school and ges-
turing with their clenched fists, shouting ob-
scenities. "Get out!"

"Go back to Europe where you came from!"

"Segregation forever!"

Terrified, I turned and ran.

I was hungry, but at the restaurant too I was turned away because of my color. "We don't want our plates dirtied by your kind!" I was told, cruelly.

Even at the little white church, to which I went for a moment's prayer, I was forbidden to enter. There too were the police, the dogs, the angry black crowds.

Could this be happening in our America, I wondered. Could there be hatred and ignorance like this? Could a man be treated no better than a beast all because of his pigmentation? And then, in a flash, I realized: It always had been happening in our country. Only now, the shoe was on the other foot.

And as the maddened crowd, brandishing a noose, tar and feathers, chains and ferocious dogs and fire hoses, closed in on me, I knew that this had been what a Great Man long ago had meant by "Do unto Others as You would have Them do unto You." For they were just treating me as they had always been treated by my friends, my forefathers, my family, by the white man.

The noose closed around my neck and...

I awoke. The alarm rang in my ears, and I had another day to begin. Another chance. Perhaps, a last chance...for all of us.

The Beginning of

the End ?

# Home Nation of Us

### Translated by Ddb́ Lẑmde Oûaejk

Most famed poemer my born country is Njalk Ghryckk
lived time (1863-19??) dead by German or Russian not sure.
Here with helping Dictionary myself make his produce
in tongue of American.  Thank you.

Inside the filled up fields with a kind of turnips
Wives of persons who pay rent make bent over working
Covered up with napkins colored spotted hair heads of
Also sweats and sings traditional folk melody rain sun is.

Answer an empire pleasing displeasing is a good advantage.
Courage the women courage the men apply ourself by them!
A library or flower eggs representing hither
Water, the waifs, eyes, bicep swimwear very green!

# The Dead Martyr

By Charles U. Farley

Down the street the big car drives,
Our handsome President still lives,
Strong and vigorous is his life,
And so is the life of his well-dressed wife.
    Cheers are loud
    In the Texas sun!
    Standing proud
    In the Texas sun!
The people all cheer, Americans all,
Not knowing he too soon will fall,
And no one in the crowd giving a shout
Hears the fatal shot ring out!
    A President dead
    In the Texas sun!
    Shot in the head
    In the Texas sun!
A Nation mourns the loss of life,
In sympathy with the glamorous wife,
His children salute their father's grave,
He died all of our lives to save!
    A solemn tune
    In the Texas sun!
    Taken too soon
    In the Texas sun!
We ask for the mad assassin's name,
Yet in a sense we are all to blame!
It is for us determined to be,
To keep our country strong and free!
    The eagle flies
    In the Texas sun!
    Through starry skies
    In the Texas sun!

# Untitled

By Ursula Wattersky


I ask the stars, "What means it all?"
The stars, they do not answer.
Why should such pain as mine befall?
Why poverty and cancer?
Why cannot brotherhood benign,
Regardless of race or creed,
Unite mankind?  Why must it shine,
When rainfall farmers need?


I ask the rain, "Is Life but grief?"
The rain makes no reply.
Why must the tree be stripped of leaf?
Why must all someday die?
Why cannot understanding reign,
Throughout the world around?
But neither from the stars nor rain
No answer can be found!

# 3 poems

by f l swisher

### poem

the flipped cigarette
  marks the dark
    neck of the night with
an angry scar of sparks
    strikes the street
  scatters dying
stars    like
    me

### question

why does that light bulb sear my soul?

### voyage

unborn generations

strip me of what
they had left
and unsinging my own songs

of joy?

(i guess not)

i take a smaller step

and

f

a

l

l

# The Kiss

(to T.A.C.)

By Lawrence Kroger


Thou talk not to me when we meet,
My love thou cannot see.
But yet I dream it would be sweet
To kiss the lips of thee!


'Tis said when thou with others be,
You give them all your heart.
Whatever they may say of thee,
I know that pure thou art!


Though thou would never give a kiss
To such a fool as I,
My dream of every night is this:
One kiss and then to die!

# C. Estes Kefauver High School Class of 1964

*Twelve-Year Tenth Reunion. Where'd Everybody Go?*

## Reunion Rap-Up

Well, a lot of us Kangaroos have hopped over a lot of dams and bridgeclubs since I last wrote to us all in the K.H.S. Class of '64! It hardly seems like our tenth reunion is already past us, even though it's actually been twelve years since our graduation, *and*, if you can believe it, I am writing this with the same Sheaffer refillable cartridge pen with the see-through middle and little squeezable refills that a certain **Herb "Wing-Ding" Weisenheimer**, '64, used to squeeze the ink out all over on everything when other people were trying to work.

The last time I wrote you all, you all may remember, I was writing you about your *pep club dues*, which some people have not yet paid. I regret to remind all those I failed to remind at last month's Tenth Reunion that these dues are *still owed* for the 300 pounds of rained-on crepe paper which was accidentally delivered for our 1964 Post-Graduation Senior Tea Brunch which, as those of you who attempted to attend will remember, was rained on.

*Everyone please "cough up!"* The Tenth Reunion Committee *still* owes, in addition, for extra janitorial services following the Saturday dinner-dance and disturbance at Moody Memorial Gymnasium. (I will be sending "follow-up" letters to each of you to remind you of the fun we had last month, and *your* share of the deficit—$17.50 per Kangaroo, or somebody's going to be hopping mad!)

I hate to single out "deadbeats" such as **Larry Kroger**, '64, and others, particularly at this time when we should be finding fun, not fault, in our classmates.

Fun *was* found, however, at our gala Tenth Reunion held this year because of flood or high winds the previous two years, and *this* pen says not the *least* fun of our Kangaromp was the fact that *this* year it didn't rain for twelve days or tornado, being too cold.

We certainly were all cheered to see each other of us that returned to K.H.S. and talk about those who didn't and wonder why, except for **Howard Lewis Havermeyer (1946-1963)** who is still no longer with us, of course.

The fun-packed weekend kanga-rolled to a start with an address by **Principal Humphrey J. Cornholt** in the new Kefauver Memorial

Gym Lounge. **Dr. Cornholt**'s speech, entitled "Welcome Back to Our New Gym Lounge," welcomed everyone who attended to the new gym lounge area, and said he was glad to see everyone again even if he didn't remember everyone's name anymore, including **Larry Kroger**'s, whose office is right next door to the Principal's Office and directly across from Detention Hall, where **Larry** and others spent so many memorable hot spring afternoons with the windows stuck closed.

"Hopped up" on enthusiasm for **Dr. Cornholt**'s plan to expand the Boys' Room facility, Kanga-returnees **Suzie "Fizzie" Fitzerman Lipbaum** and her attractive husband **Morey Lipbaum** assisted as Dr. Cornholt symbolically laid the first brick of the new hygiene complex.

Afterward, everyone gathered around the decorated card tables for pigs-in-blankets, "spiked" cranberry ade, and other delicious treats catered by **Fizzifood** (BRidgewater 7-6788) for a lot less than you'd think. As we waited for the cups to arrive, we learned from **Woolworth Van Husen III**'s lovely blond-streaked wife, **Snooky,** that their stay in the Dominican Republic with **Woolworth**'s father during that awful Trailer Bowl Scandal mix-up was "loads of laughs" and that everyone they met had bathrooms.

Driving to find someplace open with cups, **Woolworth** and **Snooky** further reported that the *Van Husen Recreation Vehicle Co.* was still very excited about its new line of self-propelled trailers *and* the prospect of full employment in the greater Dacron area, pending a favorable ruling on its appeal from the Federal Department of Transportation, or the Environmental Protection Agency, or the State Bureau of Motor Vehicle Safety. **Snooky** reports that Kangaroos **Chuck Farley** and **"Pinky" Albright Farley** visited them in the Dominican Republic in one of the new Van Husen campers during the height of "Trailer Bowl" inquiries, and that the test prototype vacation vehicle worked so well in the Dominican Republic, it stayed there even after everybody could come back.

Coming back to the Kefauver High lounge with the cups, we were greeted by the K.H.S. superintendent **Mr. Stanislaus Dupa,** who unlocked the door and said that everyone had left in anticipation of Saturday's events.

The next day, wile the lady Kangarettes enjoyed a performance of **Finian's Rainbow** at the Dacron Community Theater followed by a lecture on assistant directing by graduate **Forrest Lawford Swisher,** the menfolk met at the Cocky-Locky Chanticleer Room for a smoker and hijinx. A little Kangaroo told me that *much* of the hilarity was furnished by **Herb Weisenheimer,** who did an imitation of himself doing his auto dealership local T.V. commercial that all of us see on late nite television, only this time with more sophisticated jokes.

At the gala "Corn Ball" held that evening at the K.H.S. Moody Memorial Gymnasium, the first fox-trot of the evening was led off by **Chuck Farley** and **Woolworth**'s lovely blond-streaked wife **Snooky**, who planned the theme of the dance with **Pinky**, despite many other suggested alternatives. (**Chuck**'s face was a common appearance on Dacron telephone poles last November during his recent unsuccessful bid for block association president, and it continued to smile throughout the evening.)

After a scrumptious Fizzifood dinner in the gym lounge, over which **Frank Furter** said grace just like the American Indians did with **Faun Rosenberg**, local Dacron artist-in-residential-district, playing the part of the Great Spirit in a beautiful, feathered creation of her own creation, we all bounced back into the gym for further fun.

As K.H.S. music instructor **Mr. Dwight Mannsburden** and **Naomi "Eggy" Eggenschwiler** led off the high-hopping with a jazzy Charleston, returning Kangaroos **Vincent** and **Emily "Preggers" Lambretta** showed pictures of their six lovely children to *hardly*capped **Ursula "Wobbles" Wattersky**, who in turn showed them to her escort **Rufus Leaking**, explaining each photograph clearly and distinctly.

After **Ursula** suggested exchanging dance partners and the **Lambrettas** realized the sitter was waiting, Kangaroos throughout the gym were surprised by a special Peace Dance to Kahoutek performed by **Frank Furter** in the middle of the floor, even after the band, **Rudy Noonan and the Golden Oldsters**, stopped playing. During the intermission, little gatherings of old friends exchanged gossip and news. A popular topic of conversation was the new movie starring our own **Amana "Fridge" Peppridge**, now showing at Ray's Adult Bookmart in downtown Dacron. **Amana** says she plays a nurse, only the hospital is "less realistic" than the one on "Medical Center."

Over the years, many had lost touch with **Belinda "MetalMouth" Heinke** (now **Mrs. Hubert Howzenhower**), but were gratified to learn that her years of burning the midnight oil paid off in a fine career at McKinley Elementary School, where she unfortunately was working late Saturday night grading her students' leaf and weed collections. Those who missed her all wish her a warm "hi!"

Everyone was also happy to see **"Eggy" Eggenschwiler** and listen to her fascinating stories of what they do to you if you join Reverend Moon. Those of us who bought her magazines will certainly be glad to read or borrow them soon. We were also certainly glad to see **"Mr. Beep-Beep"** still chugging along, despite the many informative bumper stickers and Oriental shapes painted on the hubcaps.

In addition, we hope to see **"Mr. Beep-Beep"** and the rest of our autos that were found missing from the parking lot later than evening. The thefts were discovered, as you may remember, by **Carl "Fungus" Lepper**, who was escorting **Bruno Grozniac**, following an alleged disturbance, into an unmarked police car which wasn't there. Fellow Joint Narcotics Strike Force officers luckily arriving on the scene to assist **Carl** with **Bruno** were unable to locate the missing cars, as you probably know if you were there, and neither could **Dominic "Dom" Brocolli** or **Purdy "Psycho" Spackle**, who were supposed to be parking them.

It has also yet to be explained why the only vehicle not stolen was **Woolworth**'s customized Van Husen Mobile Motel, but as of this writing **Detective McNab** assures us that someone is working on it. **Detective McNab** also asked me to extend to us all his deepest concern for the loss of all our cars and don't call him anymore. He'll notify us, promises **Detective McNab**.

Well, while most of us Kangaroos filled out police forms and waited for busses in front of the closed school building that memorably nippy night, *some* of us were invited to share **Woolworth** and **Snooky**'s spacious camper with **Chuck** and **Pinky** after a quick nightcap at *Anybody's*, a very convivial gathering place for couples only, located opposite the Cocky-Locky Motel, where they refused room service the next morning to people without luggage.

Sunday morning was even more event-filled for those of us who had transportation to the final dinner-brunch held back at Moody Memorial Gym. (Yours truly still feels simply *crushed* about arriving too late to oversee the broiling of the breakfast fritters, but the poor turnout, including **Madison "Zippy" Jones** and the same government person who came back later and cut the picture of **Gilbert "Univac" Scrabbler** out of every single Reunion Ten Year Book at the Kwik-Print, meant tasty, unburnt fritters for all who wanted them.

So it was that had anyone been there besides me, my husband **Morey Lipbaum, Madison** (who says "hi!"), and the help, we all might have wished each other another fond kanga-round-of-applause for getting together again.

Good-bye for now, and C U kanga-really soon!

Busily,

Suzie "Fizzie" Lipbaum

P.S. *Don't* forget your *dos*. (Dues.)

| Madeline Beresford | Matthew Hall | Eugene Norden | Audrey Weiss |
| Michael Franks | Joseph Illiano | Terri Norden | Lucas Sotillo |
| Deborah Gerard | Diane Isenberg | Margot Rubinstein | Jonathan Weisgal |
| Neal Gilbert | Karen Nones | Philip Ruskin | Patsy Jospe |
| Jeffrey Haberman | Margot Nones | James Schnell | Nancy Horowitz |

## as members of the student body

Cheerleaders on the cover played by **Roberta Caplan, Celia Bau,** and **Laura Singer**
A.F.S. Family played by **John, Miriam,** and **Amy Richardson**
Kitchen Staff played by **Francine Rini, Patricia Torres,** and **Kathleen Tully**
Custodial Engineers played by **Christopher Cerf** and **Ernie Gilbert**

# Edited by P.J. O'Rourke and Doug Kenney
# Art Director: David Kaestle
Stylist and Production Coordinator: **Laura Singer**

Photographer: **David Kaestle**
Assistant Photographer: **Robert Parker**
Written and directed by **P.J. O'Rourke** and **Doug Kenney**
with
*Leaf and Squib* literary magazine by **Sean Kelly**
*Prism* sports pages by **Christopher Cerf**
Principal's Letter, "In Memorium" by **Ed Subitzky**
Alma Mater by **Timothy Mayer**
Poem "Voyage" by **George W.S. Trow**
Ideas and suggestions from **Michael O'Donoghue, Henry Beard, Gerald
   Sussman, George Trow, Emily Prager,** and **Matty Simmons**
Copy Editor: **Louise Gikow**
Stylists: **Lani Bergstein, Janis Hirsch, Celia Bau**
Cover photo by **Vince Aiosa**
Cover art by **Alan Rose** and **Marc Arceneaux**
Designers: **David Kaestle, Alan Rose, Marc Arceneaux,** and **Michael Gross**
Graphics by **Alan Rose, Marc Arceneaux,** and **Warren Sattler**
Additional photography by **Vince Aiosa, Alan Rose, Michael Gross,
   Dick Frank,** and **Laura Singer**
Hairstyling by **Michael Stevens, Ronnie Stevens, Louise
   Stevens, Jane,** and *Superhair*
Textbook cover illustration by **Mara McAfee**
Class ring rendering by **Wendell Robinson**

O'Rourke    Singer    Kaestle    Kenney

Black and white photo retouching by
**Egelston Retouching**

Color photo retouching by
**Tulio Martin Studios**

Custom photo finishing by
**Betsy Paffett**

Stock photographic and
illustrative material from
**UPI, Globe Photos, Frederic Lewis, Inc.,
Irwin Kramer Photography,** and the
**Bettmann Archives**

# starring

**Susan Franks** as Patricia Ann Albright
**Julian Glyck** as Robert Baxter, Jr.
**Frank Ficalora** as Dominic Xavier Brocolli
**Tracy Calvan** as Tammy Ann Croup
**Nora Mann** as Wendy Ann Dempler
**Mark Weinstein** as Charles Ulmer Farley
**Sarah Schoen** as Suzi Fitzerman
**Jay Blatt** as Franklin George Furter
**Amy Holof** as Naomi Eggenschwiler
**Steven Schonholz** as Bruno Grozniak
**Dana Cămuescu** as Belinda Heinke
**Eric Stinson** as Madison Avenue Jones
**Matthew Tendler** as Larry Kroger
**Felicia Greenfield** as Penelope Lynn Cuntz
**Paul Kaplan** as Vincent Anthony Lambretta
**Richard Weinstein** as Rufus Leaking
**Richard Young** as Carl S. Lepper
**Rachael Pine** as Ddb̉ Lžmdc Oûaejk
**Robin-Eve Jasper** as Francine Paluka
**Karin Lindroos** as Amana Peppridge
**Amy Adler** as Emily May Praeger
**Jane Kappell** as Faun Rosenberg
**Andrew Maran** as Gilbert Scrabbler
**Jon Meyersohn** as Purdy Lee Spackle
**Mark Friedman** as Maria Teresa Spermatozoa
**Jill Hellman** as Angelina Annamaria Staccato
**Gregg Adler** as Forrest Lawford Swisher
**David A. Honig** as Woolworth Van Husen III
**Janis E. Hirsch** as Ursula Wattersky
**Andrew Friend** as Herbert Leonard Weisenheimer

**Len Mogel** as Dr. Humphrey C. Cornholt
**Ted Nordman** as Mr. Martin Hackle
**Alan Rose** as Mr. Rudolph Lutz
**Howard Jurofsky** as Mr. Calvin Sneedler
**Sue Leonard** as Mrs. Evelyn Hampster
**P. J. O'Rourke** as Mr. Curtis Dittwiley
**Laura Singer** as Miss Dolores Panatella
**Nat Manes** as Mr. Dewey Fingerhuth
**Doug Kenney** as Mr. Duane Postum
**Edythe Tomkinson** as Mrs. Edith Girkins
**Brian McConnachie** as Mr. Dwight Mannsburden
**Jane Gartenberg** as Miss Mara Schweinfleisch
**Sue Katz** as Mrs. Elsa Butterick
**Louis DeGracia** as Mr. Horace Bohack
**Louise Gikow** as Mrs. Olive Finch
**Rudolph Sittler** as Coach Vernon Wormer
**P. J. O'Rourke** as Miss Marilyn Armbruster
**Lani Bergstein** as Miss Violet Coolidge
**Ed Brennan** as Swim Team Coach
**Albert Katins** as Basketball Referee
**Bob Michelson** as Wrestling Referee
**Mrs. M. Meyersohn** as Prom Chaperon
**Adrian Becker** as College Counselor
**Marvin Terban** as Football Team Doctor
**Robert Scott** as "Mill Street Murderers"
    Gang Member
**Mary Travers** as Mary Travers

Third Edition, June, 1976.
First Printing, June, 1974.
Second Printing, July, 1974.